GO!

with

Basic Computer Concepts
Getting Started

Shelley Gaskin and Victor Giol

Prentice Hall

Boston   Columbus   Indianapolis   New York   San Francisco   Upper Saddle River
Amsterdam   Cape Town   Dubai   London   Madrid   Milan   Munich   Paris   Montreal   Toronto
Delhi   Mexico City   Sao Paulo   Sydney   Hong Kong   Seoul   Singapore   Taipei   Tokyo

Editor in Chief: Michael Payne
Associate VP/Executive Acquisitions Editor, Print: Stephanie Wall
Product Development Manager: Eileen Bien Calabro
Editorial Project Manager: Laura Burgess
Development Editor: Ginny Munroe
Editorial Assistant: Nicole Sam
Director of Marketing: Kate Valentine
Marketing Manager: Tori Olson Alves
Marketing Coordinator: Susan Osterlitz
Marketing Assistant: Darshika Vyas
Senior Managing Editor: Cynthia Zonneveld
Associate Managing Editor: Camille Trentacoste
Production Project Manager: Mike Lackey
Operations Director: Alexis Heydt
Operations Specialist: Natacha Moore
Senior Art Director: Jonathan Boylan
Text and Cover Designer: Blair Brown
Cover Photo: © Ben Durrant
Manager, Visual Research: Beth Brenzel

Manager, Rights and Permissions: Zina Arabia
Photo Research Specialist: David Tietz
Image Permission Coordinator: Richard Rodrigues
Manager, Cover Visual Research & Permissions: Karen Sanatar
Rights and Permissions Manager: Shannon Barbe
Text Permissions Researcher: Christie Barros
AVP/Director of Online Programs, Media: Richard Keaveny
AVP/Director of Product Development, Media: Lisa Strite
Product Development Manager, Media: Cathi Profitko
Media Project Manager, Editorial: Alana Coles
Media Project Manager, Production: John Cassar
Supplements Editor: Craig Swanson
Full-Service Project Management: GGS Higher Education Resources, a Division of Premedia Global, Inc.
Composition: GGS Higher Education Resources, a Division of Premedia Global, Inc.
Printer/Binder: Courier/Kendallville
Cover Printer: Lehigh-Phoenix Color/Hagerstown
Text Font: Bookman Light

Credits and acknowledgments borrowed from other sources and reproduced, with permission, in this textbook are as follows or appear on appropriate page within text.

1-02a: Shutterstock; 1-02b: Robert Milek/Shutterstock; 1-02c: Timothy Passmore/Shutterstock; 1-02d; Shutterstock; 1-02e: Shutterstock: 1-02f: KariDesign/Shutterstock; 1-02g: Péter Gudella/Shutterstock; 1-02h: Shutterstock; 1-03b: Shutterstock; 1-03c: Shutterstock: 1-03d: Johanna Goodyear/Shutterstock; 1-03e: Murat BoyluShutterstock; 1-04: Shutterstock; 1-05: Shutterstock; 1-06: iStockphoto; 1-07: Antony Nettle; 1-09a: Logitech Inc.; 1-09b: Ryan McVay/ Getty Images, Inc.- -Photodisc/Royalty Free; 1-09c: Mau Horng/Shutterstock; 1-09D: Logitech Inc.; 1-10a: AMD, the AMD Arrow logo, AMD Opteron, AMD Athlon and combinations thereof, are trademarks of Advanced Micro Devices, Inc.; 1-10B: Courtesy of Intel Corporation; 1-11: Shutterstock; 1-13a: Thomas Langer/AP Wide World Photos; 1-13b: Viktor Gmyria/Shutterstock; 1-14a: Courtesy Epson America, Inc. & Mercier Wimberg Photography; 1-14b: Shutterstock; 1-14c: Konstantin Shevtsov/Shutterstock; 1-14d: Shutterstock; 1-14e: Shutterstock; 1-14f: Shutterstock; 1-16: LightScribe/Hewlett Packard; 1-17: Certance; 1-33: S. Lyudmila/Shutterstock; 1-33a: Raymond Kasprzak\Shutterstock; 1-33b: Georgios Alexandris/Shutterstock.

Microsoft® and Windows® are registered trademarks of the Microsoft Corporation in the U.S.A. and other countries. Screen shots and icons reprinted with permission from the Microsoft Corporation. This book is not sponsored or endorsed by or affiliated with the Microsoft Corporation.

Library of Congress Cataloging-in-Publication Data
CIP data on file.

10 9 8 7 6 5 4

Prentice Hall
is an imprint of

www.pearsonhighered.com

ISBN-10: 0-13-509901-3
ISBN-13: 978-0-13-509901-8

Contents

GO! System Contributors

We thank the following people for their hard work and support in making the *GO!* System all that it is!

Instructor Resource Authors

Boito, Nancy	Harrisburg Area Community College
Faix, Dennis	Harrisburg Area Community College
Nowakowski, Tony	Buffalo State
Volker, Bonita	Tidewater Community College

Technical Editors

Janice Snyder
Janet Pickard
John Traenkenschuh

Student Reviewers

Albinda, Sarah Evangeline	Phoenix College
Allen, John	Asheville-Buncombe Tech Community College
Alexander, Steven	St. Johns River Community College
Alexander, Melissa	Tulsa Community College
Bolz, Stephanie	Northern Michigan University
Berner, Ashley	Central Washington University
Boomer, Michelle	Northern Michigan University
Busse, Brennan	Northern Michigan University
Butkey, Maura	Central Washington University
Cates, Concita	Phoenix College
Charles, Marvin	Harrisburg Area Community College
Christensen, Kaylie	Northern Michigan University
Clark, Glen D. III	Harrisburg Area Community College
Cobble, Jan N.	Greenville Technical College
Connally, Brianna	Central Washington University
Davis, Brandon	Northern Michigan University
Davis, Christen	Central Washington University
De Jesus Garcia, Maria	Phoenix College
Den Boer, Lance	Central Washington University
Dix, Jessica	Central Washington University
Moeller, Jeffrey	Northern Michigan University
Downs, Elizabeth	Central Washington University
Elser, Julie	Harrisburg Area Community College
Erickson, Mike	Ball State University
Frye, Alicia	Phoenix College
Gadomski, Amanda	Northern Michigan University
Gassert, Jennifer	Harrisburg Area Community College
Gross, Mary Jo	Kirkwood Community College
Gyselinck, Craig	Central Washington University
Harrison, Margo	Central Washington University
Hatt, Patrick	Harrisburg Area Community College
Heacox, Kate	Central Washington University
Hedgman, Shaina	Tidewater College
Hill, Cheretta	Northwestern State University
Hochstedler, Bethany	Harrisburg Area Community College Lancaster
Homer, Jean	Greenville Technical College
Innis, Tim	Tulsa Community College
Jarboe, Aaron	Central Washington University
Key, Penny	Greenville Technical College
Klein, Colleen	Northern Michigan University
Lloyd, Kasey	Ivy Tech Bloomington
Moeller, Jeffrey	Northern Michigan University
Mullen, Sharita	Tidewater Community College
Nelson, Cody	Texas Tech University
Nicholson, Regina	Athens Tech College
Niehaus, Kristina	Northern Michigan University
Nisa, Zaibun	Santa Rosa Community College
Nunez, Nohelia	Santa Rosa Community College
Oak, Samantha	Central Washington University
Oberly, Sara	Harrisburg Area Community College Lancaster
Oertii, Monica	Central Washington University
Palenshus, Juliet	Central Washington University
Pohl, Amanda	Northern Michigan University
Presnell, Randy	Central Washington University
Reed, Kailee	Texas Tech University
Ritner, April	Northern Michigan University
Roberts, Corey	Tulsa Community College
Rodgers, Spencer	Texas Tech University
Rodriguez, Flavia	Northwestern State University
Rogers, A.	Tidewater Community College
Rossi, Jessica Ann	Central Washington University
Rothbauer, Taylor	Trident Technical College
Rozelle, Lauren	Texas Tech University
Schmadeke, Kimberly	Kirkwood Community College
Shafapay, Natasha	Central Washington University
Shanahan, Megan	Northern Michigan University
Sullivan, Alexandra Nicole	Greenville Technical College
Teska, Erika	Hawaii Pacific University
Torrenti, Natalie	Harrisburg Area Community College
Traub, Amy	Northern Michigan University
Underwood, Katie	Central Washington University
Walters, Kim	Central Washington University
Warren, Jennifer L.	Greenville Technical College
Wilson, Kelsie	Central Washington University
Wilson, Amanda	Green River Community College
Wylie, Jimmy	Texas Tech University

Contributors continued

Series Reviewers

Abraham, Reni — Houston Community College
Addison, Paul — Ivy Tech Community College
Agatston, Ann — Agatston Consulting Technical College
Akuna, Valeria, Ph.D. — Estrella Mountain Community College
Alexander, Melody — Ball Sate University
Alejandro, Manuel — Southwest Texas Junior College
Alger, David — Tidewater Community College Chesapeake Campus
Allen, Jackie — Rowan-Cabarrus Community College
Ali, Farha — Lander University
Amici, Penny — Harrisburg Area Community College
Anderson, Patty A. — Lake City Community College
Andrews, Wilma — Virginia Commonwealth College, Nebraska University
Anik, Mazhar — Tiffin University
Armstrong, Gary — Shippensburg University
Arnold, Linda L. — Harrisburg Area Community College
Ashby, Tom — Oklahoma City Community College
Atkins, Bonnie — Delaware Technical Community College
Aukland, Cherie — Thomas Nelson Community College
Bachand, LaDonna — Santa Rosa Community College
Bagui, Sikha — University of West Florida
Beecroft, Anita — Kwantlen University College
Bell, Paula — Lock Haven College
Belton, Linda — Springfield Tech. Community College
Bennett, Judith — Sam Houston State University
Bhatia, Sai — Riverside Community College
Bishop, Frances — DeVry Institute—Alpharetta (ATL)
Blaszkiewicz, Holly — Ivy Tech Community College/Region 1
Boito, Nancy — HACC Central Pennsylvania's Community College
Borger-Boglin, Grietje L. — San Antonio College/Northeast Lakeview College
Branigan, Dave — DeVry University
Bray, Patricia — Allegany College of Maryland
Britt, Brenda K. — Fayetteville Technical Community College
Brotherton, Cathy — Riverside Community College
Brown, Judy — Western Illinois University
Buehler, Lesley — Ohlone College
Buell, C — Central Oregon Community College
Burns, Christine — Central New Mexico Community College
Byars, Pat — Brookhaven College
Byrd, Julie — Ivy Tech Community College
Byrd, Lynn — Delta State University, Cleveland, Mississippi
Cacace, Richard N. — Pensacola Junior College
Cadenhead, Charles — Brookhaven College
Calhoun, Ric — Gordon College
Cameron, Eric — Passaic Community College
Canine, Jill — Ivy Tech Community College of Indiana

Cannamore, Madie — Kennedy King
Cannon, Kim — Greenville Technical College
Carreon, Cleda — Indiana University—Purdue University, Indianapolis
Carriker, Sandra — North Shore Community College
Casey, Patricia — Trident Technical College
Cates, Wally — Central New Mexico Community College
Chaffin, Catherine — Shawnee State University
Chauvin, Marg — Palm Beach Community College, Boca Raton
Challa, Chandrashekar — Virginia State University
Chamlou, Afsaneh — NOVA Alexandria
Chapman, Pam — Wabaunsee Community College
Christensen, Dan — Iowa Western Community College
Clay, Betty — Southeastern Oklahoma State University
Collins, Linda D. — Mesa Community College
Cone, Bill — Northern Arizona University
Conroy-Link, Janet — Holy Family College
Conway, Ronald — Bowling Green State University
Cornforth, Carol G. — WVNCC
Cosgrove, Janet — Northwestern CT Community
Courtney, Kevin — Hillsborough Community College
Coverdale, John — Riverside Community College
Cox, Rollie — Madison Area Technical College
Crawford, Hiram — Olive Harvey College
Crawford, Sonia — Central New Mexico Community College
Crawford, Thomasina — Miami-Dade College, Kendall Campus
Credico, Grace — Lethbridge Community College
Crenshaw, Richard — Miami Dade Community College, North
Crespo, Beverly — Mt. San Antonio College
Crooks, Steven — Texas Tech University
Crossley, Connie — Cincinnati State Technical Community College
Curik, Mary — Central New Mexico Community College
De Arazoza, Ralph — Miami Dade Community College
Danno, John — DeVry University/Keller Graduate School
Davis, Phillip — Del Mar College
Davis, Richard — Trinity Valley Community College
Davis, Sandra — Baker College of Allen Park
Dees, Stephanie D. — Wharton County Junior College
DeHerrera, Laurie — Pikes Peak Community College
Delk, Dr. K. Kay — Seminole Community College
Denton, Bree — Texas Tech University
Dix, Jeanette — Ivy Tech Community College
Dooly, Veronica P. — Asheville-Buncombe Technical Community College
Doroshow, Mike — Eastfield College
Douglas, Gretchen — SUNYCortland
Dove, Carol — Community College of Allegheny
Dozier, Susan — Tidewater Community College, Virginia Beach Campus
Driskel, Loretta — Niagara Community College
Duckwiler, Carol — Wabaunsee Community College
Duhon, David — Baker College
Duncan, Mimi — University of Missouri-St. Louis
Duthie, Judy — Green River Community College

Duvall, Annette	Central New Mexico Community College
Ecklund, Paula	Duke University
Eilers, Albert	Cincinnati State Technical and Community College
Eng, Bernice	Brookdale Community College
Epperson, Arlin	Columbia College
Evans, Billie	Vance-Granville Community College
Evans, Jean	Brevard Community College
Feuerbach, Lisa	Ivy Tech East Chicago
Finley, Jean	ABTCC
Fisher, Fred	Florida State University
Foster, Nancy	Baker College
Foster-Shriver, Penny L.	Anne Arundel Community College
Foster-Turpen, Linda	CNM
Foszcz, Russ	McHenry County College
Fry, Susan	Boise State University
Fustos, Janos	Metro State
Gallup, Jeanette	Blinn College
Gelb, Janet	Grossmont College
Gentry, Barb	Parkland College
Gerace, Karin	St. Angela Merici School
Gerace, Tom	Tulane University
Ghajar, Homa	Oklahoma State University
Gifford, Steve	Northwest Iowa Community College
Glazer, Ellen	Broward Community College
Gordon, Robert	Hofstra University
Gramlich, Steven	Pasco-Hernando Community College
Graviett, Nancy M.	St. Charles Community College, St. Peters, Missouri
Greene, Rich	Community College of Allegheny County
Gregoryk, Kerry	Virginia Commonwealth State
Griggs, Debra	Bellevue Community College
Grimm, Carol	Palm Beach Community College
Guthrie, Rose	Fox Valley Technical College
Hahn, Norm	Thomas Nelson Community College
Haley-Hunter, Deb	Bluefield State College
Hall, Linnea	Northwest Mississippi Community College
Hammerschlag, Dr. Bill	Brookhaven College
Hansen, Michelle	Davenport University
Hayden, Nancy	Indiana University—Purdue University, Indianapolis
Hayes, Theresa	Broward Community College
Headrick, Betsy	Chattanooga State
Helfand, Terri	Chaffey College
Helms, Liz	Columbus State Community College
Hernandez, Leticia	TCI College of Technology
Hibbert, Marilyn	Salt Lake Community College
Hinds, Cheryl	Norfolk State University
Hines, James	Tidewater Community College
Hoffman, Joan	Milwaukee Area Technical College
Hogan, Pat	Cape Fear Community College
Holland, Susan	Southeast Community College
Holliday, Mardi	Community College of Philadelphia
Hollingsworth, Mary Carole	Georgia Perimeter College
Hopson, Bonnie	Athens Technical College
Horvath, Carrie	Albertus Magnus College
Horwitz, Steve	Community College of Philadelphia
Hotta, Barbara	Leeward Community College
Howard, Bunny	St. Johns River Community
Howard, Chris	DeVry University
Huckabay, Jamie	Austin Community College
Hudgins, Susan	East Central University
Hulett, Michelle J.	Missouri State University
Humphrey, John	Asheville Buncombe Technical Community College
Hunt, Darla A.	Morehead State University, Morehead, Kentucky
Hunt, Laura	Tulsa Community College
Ivey, Joan M.	Lanier Technical College
Jacob, Sherry	Jefferson Community College
Jacobs, Duane	Salt Lake Community College
Jauken, Barb	Southeastern Community
Jerry, Gina	Santa Monica College
Johnson, Deborah S.	Edison State College
Johnson, Kathy	Wright College
Johnson, Mary	Kingwood College
Johnson, Mary	Mt. San Antonio College
Jones, Stacey	Benedict College
Jones, Warren	University of Alabama, Birmingham
Jordan, Cheryl	San Juan College
Kapoor, Bhushan	California State University, Fullerton
Kasai, Susumu	Salt Lake Community College
Kates, Hazel	Miami Dade Community College, Kendall
Keen, Debby	University of Kentucky
Keeter, Sandy	Seminole Community College
Kern-Blystone, Dorothy Jean	Bowling Green State
Kerwin, Annette	College of DuPage
Keskin, Ilknur	The University of South Dakota
Kinney, Mark B.	Baker College
Kirk, Colleen	Mercy College
Kisling, Eric	East Carolina University
Kleckner, Michelle	Elon University
Kliston, Linda	Broward Community College, North Campus
Knuth, Toni	Baker College of Auburn Hills
Kochis, Dennis	Suffolk County Community College
Kominek, Kurt	Northeast State Technical Community College
Kramer, Ed	Northern Virginia Community College
Kretz, Daniel	Fox Valley Technical College
Laird, Jeff	Northeast State Community College
Lamoureaux, Jackie	Central New Mexico Community College
Lange, David	Grand Valley State
LaPointe, Deb	Central New Mexico Community College
Larsen, Jacqueline Anne	A-B Tech
Larson, Donna	Louisville Technical Institute
Laspina, Kathy	Vance-Granville Community College
Le Grand, Dr. Kate	Broward Community College
Lenhart, Sheryl	Terra Community College

Leonard, Yvonne	Coastal Carolina Community College	McLeod, Todd	Fresno City College
Letavec, Chris	University of Cincinnati	McManus, Illyana	Grossmont College
Lewis, Daphne L, Ed.D.	Wayland Baptist University	McPherson, Dori	Schoolcraft College
Lewis, Julie	Baker College-Allen Park	Meck, Kari	HACC
Liefert, Jane	Everett Community College	Meiklejohn, Nancy	Pikes Peak Community College
Lindaman, Linda	Black Hawk Community College	Menking, Rick	Hardin-Simmons University
Lindberg, Martha	Minnesota State University	Meredith, Mary	University of Louisiana at Lafayette
Lightner, Renee	Broward Community College		
Lindberg, Martha	Minnesota State University	Mermelstein, Lisa	Baruch College
Linge, Richard	Arizona Western College	Metos, Linda	Salt Lake Community College
Logan, Mary G.	Delgado Community College	Meurer, Daniel	University of Cincinnati
Loizeaux, Barbara	Westchester Community College	Meyer, Colleen	Cincinnati State Technical and Community College
Lombardi, John	South University		
Lopez, Don	Clovis-State Center Community College District	Meyer, Marian	Central New Mexico Community College
Lopez, Lisa	Spartanburg Community College	Miller, Cindy	Ivy Tech Community College, Lafayette, Indiana
Lord, Alexandria	Asheville Buncombe Tech		
Lovering, LeAnne	Augusta Technical College	Mills, Robert E.	Tidewater Community College, Portsmouth Campus
Lowe, Rita	Harold Washington College		
Low, Willy Hui	Joliet Junior College	Mitchell, Susan	Davenport University
Lucas, Vickie	Broward Community College	Mohle, Dennis	Fresno Community College
Luna, Debbie	El Paso Community College	Molki, Saeed	South Texas College
Luoma, Jean	Davenport University	Monk, Ellen	University of Delaware
Luse, Steven P.	Horry Georgetown Technical College	Moore, Rodney	Holland College
		Morris, Mike	Southeastern Oklahoma State University
Lynam, Linda	Central Missouri State University		
Lyon, Lynne	Durham College	Morris, Nancy	Hudson Valley Community College
Lyon, Pat Rajski	Tomball College		
Macarty, Matthew	University of New Hampshire	Moseler, Dan	Harrisburg Area Community College
MacKinnon, Ruth	Georgia Southern University		
Macon, Lisa	Valencia Community College, West Campus	Nabors, Brent	Reedley College, Clovis Center
		Nadas, Erika	Wright College
Machuca, Wayne	College of the Sequoias	Nadelman, Cindi	New England College
Mack, Sherri	Butler County Community College	Nademlynsky, Lisa	Johnson & Wales University
Madison, Dana	Clarion University	Nagengast, Joseph	Florida Career College
Maguire, Trish	Eastern New Mexico University	Nason, Scott	Rowan Cabarrus Community College
Malkan, Rajiv	Montgomery College		
Manning, David	Northern Kentucky University	Ncube, Cathy	University of West Florida
Marcus, Jacquie	Niagara Community College	Newsome, Eloise	Northern Virginia Community College Woodbridge
Marghitu, Daniela	Auburn University		
Marks, Suzanne	Bellevue Community College	Nicholls, Doreen	Mohawk Valley Community College
Marquez, Juanita	El Centro College		
Marquez, Juan	Mesa Community College	Nicholson, John R.	Johnson County Community College
Martin, Carol	Harrisburg Area Community College		
		Nielson, Phil	Salt Lake Community College
Martin, Paul C.	Harrisburg Area Community College	Nunan, Karen L.	Northeast State Technical Community College
Martyn, Margie	Baldwin-Wallace College	O'Neal, Lois Ann	Rogers State University
Marucco, Toni	Lincoln Land Community College	Odegard, Teri	Edmonds Community College
Mason, Lynn	Lubbock Christian University	Ogle, Gregory	North Community College
Matutis, Audrone	Houston Community College	Orr, Dr. Claudia	Northern Michigan University South
Matkin, Marie	University of Lethbridge		
Maurel, Trina	Odessa College	Orsburn, Glen	Fox Valley Technical College
May, Karen	Blinn College	Otieno, Derek	DeVry University
McCain, Evelynn	Boise State University	Otton, Diana Hill	Chesapeake College
McCannon, Melinda	Gordon College	Oxendale, Lucia	West Virginia Institute of Technology
McCarthy, Marguerite	Northwestern Business College		
McCaskill, Matt L.	Brevard Community College	Paiano, Frank	Southwestern College
McClellan, Carolyn	Tidewater Community College	Pannell, Dr. Elizabeth	Collin College
McClure, Darlean	College of Sequoias	Patrick, Tanya	Clackamas Community College
McCrory, Sue A.	Missouri State University	Paul, Anindya	Daytona State College
McCue, Stacy	Harrisburg Area Community College	Peairs, Deb	Clark State Community College
		Perez, Kimberly	Tidewater Community College
		Porter, Joyce	Weber State University
McEntire-Orbach, Teresa	Middlesex County College	Prince, Lisa	Missouri State University-Springfield Campus
McKinley, Lee	Georgia Perimeter College		

Contributors continued

Proietti, Kathleen	Northern Essex Community College	Steiner, Ester	New Mexico State University
Puopolo, Mike	Bunker Hill Community College	Stenlund, Neal	Northern Virginia Community College, Alexandria
Pusins, Delores	HCCC	St. John, Steve	Tulsa Community College
Putnam, Darlene	Thomas Nelson Community College	Sterling, Janet	Houston Community College
		Stoughton, Catherine	Laramie County Community College
Raghuraman, Ram	Joliet Junior College	Sullivan, Angela	Joliet Junior College
Rani, Chigurupati	BMCC/CUNY	Sullivan, Denise	Westchester Community College
Reasoner, Ted Allen	Indiana University—Purdue	Sullivan, Joseph	Joliet Junior College
Reeves, Karen	High Point University	Swart, John	Louisiana Tech University
Remillard, Debbie	New Hampshire Technical Institute	Szurek, Joseph	University of Pittsburgh at Greensburg
Rhue, Shelly	DeVry University		
Richards, Karen	Maplewoods Community College	Taff, Ann	Tulsa Community College
Richardson, Mary	Albany Technical College	Taggart, James	Atlantic Cape Community College
Rodgers, Gwen	Southern Nazarene University	Tarver, Mary Beth	Northwestern State University
Rodie, Karla	Pikes Peak Community College	Taylor, Michael	Seattle Central Community College
Roselli, Diane Maie	Harrisburg Area Community College	Terrell, Robert L.	Carson-Newman College
Ross, Dianne	University of Louisiana in Lafayette	Terry, Dariel	Northern Virginia Community College
Rousseau, Mary	Broward Community College, South	Thangiah, Sam	Slippery Rock University
Rovetto, Ann	Horry-Georgetown Technical College	Thayer, Paul	Austin Community College
Rusin, Iwona	Baker College	Thompson, Joyce	Lehigh Carbon Community College
Sahabi, Ahmad	Baker College of Clinton Township	Thompson-Sellers, Ingrid	Georgia Perimeter College
Samson, Dolly	Hawaii Pacific University	Tomasi, Erik	Baruch College
Sams, Todd	University of Cincinnati	Toreson, Karen	Shoreline Community College
Sandoval, Everett	Reedley College	Townsend, Cynthia	Baker College
Santiago, Diana	Central New Mexico Community College	Trifiletti, John J.	Florida Community College at Jacksonville
Sardone, Nancy	Seton Hall University	Trivedi, Charulata	Quinsigamond Community College, Woodbridge
Scafide, Jean	Mississippi Gulf Coast Community College	Tucker, William	Austin Community College
Scheeren, Judy	Westmoreland County Community College	Turgeon, Cheryl	Asnuntuck Community College
		Turpen, Linda	Central New Mexico Community College
Scheiwe, Adolph	Joliet Junior College	Upshaw, Susan	Del Mar College
Schneider, Sol	Sam Houston State University	Unruh, Angela	Central Washington University
Schweitzer, John	Central New Mexico Community College	Vanderhoof, Dr. Glenna	Missouri State University-Springfield Campus
Scroggins, Michael	Southwest Missouri State University	Vargas, Tony	El Paso Community College
Sedlacek, Brenda	Tidewater Community College	Vicars, Mitzi	Hampton University
Sell, Kelly	Anne Arundel Community College	Villarreal, Kathleen	Fresno
Sever, Suzanne	Northwest Arkansas Community College	Vitrano, Mary Ellen	Palm Beach Community College
Sewell, John	Florida Career College	Vlaich-Lee, Michelle	Greenville Technical College
Sheridan, Rick	California State University-Chico	Volker, Bonita	Tidewater Community College
Silvers, Pamela	Asheville Buncombe Tech	Waddell, Karen	Butler Community College
Sindt, Robert G.	Johnson County Community College	Wahila, Lori (Mindy)	Tompkins Cortland Community College
Singer, Noah	Tulsa Community College	Wallace, Melissa	Lanier Technical College
Singer, Steven A.	University of Hawai'i, Kapi'olani Community College	Walters, Gary B.	Central New Mexico Community College
Sinha, Atin	Albany State University	Waswick, Kim	Southeast Community College, Nebraska
Skolnick, Martin	Florida Atlantic University		
Smith, Kristi	Allegany College of Maryland	Wavle, Sharon M.	Tompkins Cortland Community College
Smith, Patrick	Marshall Community and Technical College	Webb, Nancy	City College of San Francisco
Smith, Stella A.	Georgia Gwinnett College	Webb, Rebecca	Northwest Arkansas Community College
Smith, T. Michael	Austin Community College	Weber, Sandy	Gateway Technical College
Smith, Tammy	Tompkins Cortland Community Collge	Weissman, Jonathan	Finger Lakes Community College
Smolenski, Bob	Delaware County Community College	Wells, Barbara E.	Central Carolina Technical College
Smolenski, Robert	Delaware Community College	Wells, Lorna	Salt Lake Community College
Southwell, Donald	Delta College	Welsh, Jean	Lansing Community College Nebraska
Spangler, Candice	Columbus State		
Spangler, Candice	Columbus State Community College	White, Bruce	Quinnipiac University
Stark, Diane	Phoenix College	Willer, Ann	Solano Community College
Stedham, Vicki	St. Petersburg College, Clearwater	Williams, Mark	Lane Community College
Stefanelli, Greg	Carroll Community College		

Williams, Ronald D.	Central Piedmont Community College	Wright, Darrell	Shelton State Community College
Wilms, Dr. G. Jan	Union University	Wright, Julie	Baker College
Wilson, Kit	Red River College	Yauney, Annette	Herkimer County Community College
Wilson, MaryLou	Piedmont Technical College	Yip, Thomas	Passaic Community College
Wilson, Roger	Fairmont State University	Zavala, Ben	Webster Tech
Wimberly, Leanne	International Academy of Design and Technology	Zaboski, Maureen	University of Scranton
		Zlotow, Mary Ann	College of DuPage
Winters, Floyd	Manatee Community College	Zudeck, Steve	Broward Community College, North
Worthington, Paula	Northern Virginia Community College	Zullo, Matthew D.	Wake Technical Community College

About the Authors

Shelley Gaskin, Series Editor, is a professor of business and computer technology at Pasadena City College in Pasadena, California. She holds a master's degree in business education from Northern Illinois University and a doctorate in adult and community education from Ball State University. Dr. Gaskin has 15 years of experience in the computer industry with several Fortune 500 companies and has developed and written training materials for custom systems applications in both the public and private sector. She is also the author of books on Microsoft Outlook and word processing.

Victor Giol is an Associate Professor Sr. teaching for the Computer Information Systems Department at Miami Dade College. He holds a master's degree in Applications in Computer Education from Nova Southeastern University in Davie, Florida. Professor Giol has been teaching computer-related courses for over 19 years. As a tenured professor he participates in numerous campus and college-wide activities including curriculum development and new student's orientation. He also serves as the myitlab administrator for two campuses and offers training sessions for faculty and lab paraprofessionals. Victor enjoys spending time with his two children and four grandchildren and one of his favorite hobbies is playing Latin percussion instruments with a small Latin Jazz ensemble at one of the college's campuses.

To our four grandchildren, Tori, Todd, Grace, and Gabriel. May they be together as a family one day in the, not too distant, future.

—VICTOR GIOL

GO! Instructor Materials

The following instructor materials are available on either the instructors resource CD or www.pearsonhighered.com/go

Annotated Solution Files
Coupled with the assignment tags this creates a grading and scoring system that makes grading so much easier for you

Assignment Sheets
Lists all the assignments for the chapter, you just add in the course information, due dates and points. Providing these to students ensures they will know what is due and when

Point-Counted Production Tests
Exams for each chapter

Power Point Lectures
PowerPoint presentations for each chapter

Scorecards
Can be used either by students to check their work or by you as a quick check-off for the items that need to be corrected

Solution Files
Answers to the projects in the book

Scripted Lectures
Classroom lectures prepared for you

Test Bank
Includes a variety of test questions for each chapter

Companion Web Site
Online content such as the Online Study Guide, Glossary, and Student Data Files are all at www.pearsonhighered.com/go

Basic Computer Concepts

OBJECTIVES

Mastering these objectives will enable you to:

1. Define Computer and Identify the Four Basic Computing Functions (p. 2)
2. Identify the Different Types of Computers (p. 5)
3. Describe Hardware Devices and Their Uses (p. 9)
4. Identify Types of Software and Their Uses (p. 29)
5. Describe Networks and Define Network Terms (p. 40)
6. Identify Safe Computing Practices (p. 44)

In This Chapter

Computers are an integral part of our lives. They are found in homes, offices, stores, hospitals, libraries, and many other places. Computers are part of cars and phones, and they enable you to access bank accounts from home, shop online, and quickly communicate with people around the world by means of e-mail and the Internet. It is difficult to find a business or occupation that doesn't rely on computers. Whether it's a truck driver who keeps an electronic travel log or a high-powered stockbroker who needs up-to-the-second market information, computers can make these tasks faster, easier, more efficient, and more accurate.

Computers are all around us, which makes it important to learn basic computing skills and gain the knowledge to be a responsible computer user. Knowing how to use a computer makes you ***computer fluent***.

This chapter looks at different types of computers and their functions. It discusses computer hardware and software and the benefits of networking. In addition, this chapter also discusses the importance of safe computing practices and the ways that you can protect your computer from various threats.

Objective 1 | Define Computer and Identify the Four Basic Computing Functions

What are the benefits of becoming computer fluent? Becoming computer fluent can benefit you in several ways. The advantage of being computer fluent is that it makes employees more attractive to potential employers. Many employers expect employees to have basic computer skills when they are hired. Computers have certainly changed the way we work. The traditional memo has given way to e-mail messages. Business reports can now be shared on a network, enabling a group of individuals to collaborate by adding their own notes and comments before the final report is finalized. Presentations are seldom delivered via overhead transparencies; presentation graphic software is widely used to share information with an audience in a conference room or via the company's intranet. Spreadsheet software is a key tool in presenting financial information and developing sound business plans.

On the other hand, if you are knowledgeable about computers and their uses, it also makes you a better consumer. You feel more comfortable when it comes to purchasing the right computer hardware and software for your needs, adding a peripheral for a specific use, or detecting basic problems when a system does not work properly. Also, if you have a basic understanding of today's technology, you can better understand and use *new* technologies.

What are the basic functions of a computer? A **computer** is a programmable electronic device that can input, process, output, and store data. The term **programmable** signifies that a device can be instructed to perform a task or a function when fed with a program or software. A computer takes data and converts it into information. **Data** represents text, numbers, graphics, sounds, and videos entered into the computer's memory during input operations.

Information is data that has been processed so that it can be presented in an organized and meaningful way. Think of data as the pieces of a jigsaw puzzle and information as the finished puzzle. Putting the pieces of the puzzle together gives you the overall picture. For example, CIS1100, the letter B, and the name Amy Stevens are pieces of data. Individually, these pieces of data seem meaningless. However, when processed, this data becomes the information on a grade report that indicates Amy Stevens received a grade of B in her CIS 1100 class.

These four basic computer functions work in a cycle known as the ***information processing cycle***. See Figure 1.1.

The functions of this cycle are:

- ***Input***—The computer gathers data or enables a user to enter data.
- ***Process***—Data is manipulated and converted into information.
- ***Output***—Information is displayed or shown to the user in a way that is understandable.
- ***Storage***—Data and/or information is stored for future use.

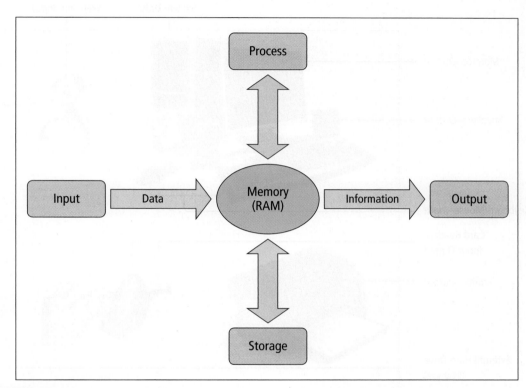

Figure 1.1

These are the four computer functions within the information processing cycle. Memory is not considered a function, but it is the center of flow of data and information within this cycle.

In the grade report, the instructor used a computer to enter, or input, the students' grades into the school's computerized grading system. A computer then processed this data along with data for other classes the students might have taken. In the example, the student Amy then received a written record of her grade or she accessed her grades online. The grade report was output by the computer. In addition, her grades remain stored in the system so they can be used to generate her transcript or to determine her future grade point average as she continues to take classes. See Figure 1.2.

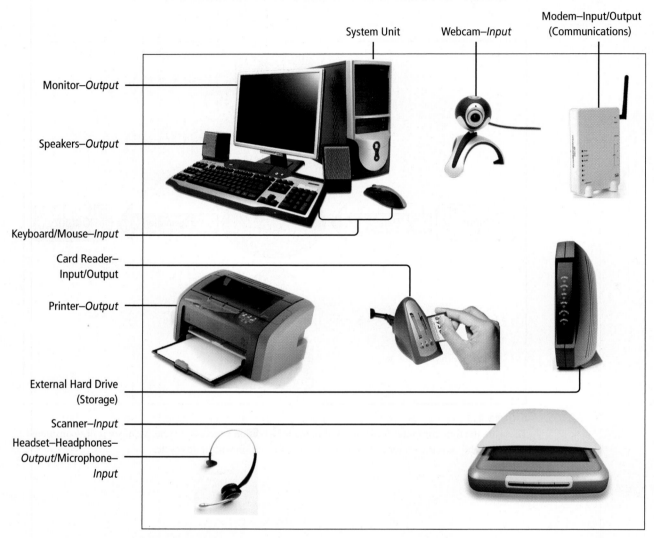

Figure 1.2
The components of a typical computer system and the appropriate step in the information processing cycle.

Objective 2 | Identify the Different Types of Computers

What are the different types of computers and what are their uses? Although computers come in a variety of sizes and shapes, the basic components required to complete the information processing cycle must be present in them. In addition to ***microcomputers***, the desktop and notebook computers and mobile devices that many of us are familiar with, there are also specialty computers, including servers, mainframes, supercomputers, and embedded computers. See Figure 1.3.

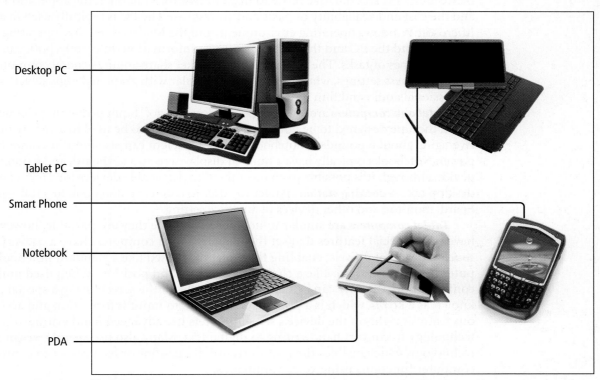

Desktop PC

Tablet PC

Smart Phone

Notebook

PDA

Figure 1.3
Types of microcomputers

Microcomputers

What are microcomputers? The term microcomputer means that the main component of a computer is a microprocessor, a tiny but powerful chip that is very small in size compared to a mainframe or a supercomputer. Microcomputers are classified as small, inexpensive, and designed for personal use or as part of a network of computers in a business environment. Computers in this category range in size from a desktop size system that is ideal when portability is not required to handheld devices that fit in your pocket. Some of the most common types of microcomputers include the following:

- ***Desktop computers*** are computers that sit on the desk, floor, or table, and typically have a detachable keyboard, mouse, monitor, and possibly other peripheral devices, such as digital cameras, scanners, and music players. Desktop computers are used in most homes and in business applications where portability is not needed. They can be configured in a multitude of arrangements depending on the specific needs and budget constraints. To ***configure*** means to put together by selecting a specific combination of components, features, and options.

- ***Gaming computers*** are mostly used by video game enthusiasts. They are usually configured with a fast CPU, large amount of memory, a special video card, joystick or game pad, and sound card with surround sound speaker system.

Desktop computers generally fall into two main categories: PCs or Macs. The PC, or personal computer, originally referred to as the IBM personal computer when it was released in the early 1980s, is now manufactured by a variety of companies including Hewlett-Packard, Dell, and Gateway. Today the term *PC* applies to any personal computer based on an Intel microprocessor, or on an Intel-compatible microprocessor. The Apple Macintosh computer, now known as Mac, is manufactured exclusively by Apple Inc. with an Intel microprocessor and can perform the same functions as the PC.

There are pros and cons to both types of computers, but in reality, both are good systems and the choice usually comes down to personal preference. The primary differences between the PC and the Mac relate to the different user interface, the application software, and the cost and availability of parts and accessories. The PC is typically used in a Microsoft Windows operating environment, and the Mac uses the Mac operating system. Although and the PC and the Mac each process information differently, both can perform the same types of tasks. The PC has a larger market share among general computer users and in business settings, whereas the Mac is popular with graphic design, advertising, and professional audio and film industries.

Notebook computers are ideal for people "on-the-go." Equipped with rechargeable batteries, they are designed to be portable, permitting them to be used in a variety of places. Averaging about 6 pounds, a notebook's size and weight can also limit its computing power. Notebooks typically have a built-in display screen, a keyboard, and a pointing device, although it is possible to connect them to detachable devices for more comfortable desktop use. A ***docking station*** enables the user to connect a notebook to a full-size keyboard, monitor, and other devices in an office setting.

Tablet computers are similar to notebooks because they are portable; however, they have some special features that set them apart. Tablet computers have a convertible ***touch screen*** that swivels, enabling the tablet to be used like a standard notebook computer in one position or like a clipboard in the second position. When used in the tablet configuration, the user can actually write directly on the screen using a special pen known as a ***stylus***, which is a pointed device used to input information and access various features right on the device's screen. Tablets use advanced handwriting-recognition technology to convert handwriting to digital text. Many also use ***speech-recognition*** technology, which enables the user to record discussions or lectures, or to control the computer functions using voice commands.

Mobile devices include items such as ***personal digital assistants (PDAs)***, ***handheld computers*** (Pocket PCs), and ***smartphones***. These devices vary in size and purpose, but they are all ultra-lightweight and portable. PDAs were initially designed to provide a convenient resource for maintaining an organized calendar and list of business and personal associates. Handheld computers enable users to access personal productivity software and send e-mail over the Internet, while smartphones add Internet capability to the wireless communication aspects of cell phones.

The newest mobile devices are often referred to simply as "handhelds." Many handheld devices now include personal productivity software and enable the user to play music, take photos and video, make phone calls, and access the Internet. PDAs and Pocket PCs often use a stylus. It is not uncommon for these devices to use a small detachable keyboard for text and data entry. As the features of mobile devices continue to converge, permitting them to perform similar tasks, it becomes more difficult to differentiate between them. If you are in the process of buying one of these handhelds, you need to do some research and make sure that you get the features and functions you want.

Servers

What are servers? When computers are connected together in a ***network*** environment, ***servers*** are specialized computers that manage network resources through the use of administrative software (see Figure 1.4). They provide other computers with access to the network and can handle a variety of functions or may be assigned to just one particular type of task. Thus, within the same company, you might find a Web server that holds and delivers the organization's Web pages, a file server that handles the storage and retrieval tasks for all of the company's files, and a printer server that handles all print requests. Also, virtual servers (not real, but an abstraction) can manage other specialized servers without the added cost of additional hardware.

Figure 1.4
Network server

What are mainframe computers? Mainframe computers are large computers often found in large businesses, organizations, and government agencies where thousands of users need to simultaneously use the data and resources of their institution (see Figure 1.5). Mainframe computers ***multitask***; that is, they can perform more than one task at a time. Mainframes can store vast amounts of data using a variety of storage. Mainframes are often used for high-security applications, bulk data processing such as data surveys and census, and statistics. Early mainframe computers were very large and required separate rooms to house them, while today's mainframes are significantly smaller, faster, and more powerful than their predecessors.

Figure 1.5
Mainframe computer

Supercomputers

What are supercomputers? Supercomputers are large, powerful, and ultrafast computers that perform specialized tasks. Some of these are used for research, processing intensive scientific calculations, and multi-scale simulations. Since June 2008, the IBM nicknamed "Roadrunner," at the Department of Energy's Los Alamos National Laboratory in New Mexico, holds top spot as the world's fastest supercomputer. (See http://www.top500.org/ for more information about Roadrunner.)

Supercomputers (see Figure 1.6) are the fastest and most expensive computers. Unlike a mainframe computer that can handle a number of programs simultaneously, the supercomputer is designed to run fewer programs at one time, but to do so as quickly as possible. They perform sophisticated mathematical calculations, track weather patterns, monitor satellites, and perform other complex, dedicated tasks.

Figure 1.6
Supercomputer

Embedded Computers

What are embedded computers? ***Embedded computers*** are small specialized computers built into larger components such as automobiles and appliances. Functions such as emission control systems, antilock braking systems (ABS), airbags, and stability control systems are common in today's vehicles. These computers use a specially programmed microprocessor to perform a set of predefined tasks, and may require little or no input from the user. Other examples include electronic appliances, microwave ovens, digital cameras, programmable thermostats, medical devices, and diagnostic equipment.

Objective 3 | Describe Hardware Devices and Their Uses

What is computer hardware? ***Hardware*** is the computer and any equipment connected to it. Hardware devices are the physical components of the computer. Items such as the monitor, keyboard, mouse, and printer are also known as ***peripherals*** because they attach to the computer. In Figure 1.3, the computer and different peripherals are matched with the individual steps of the information processing cycle.

The computer itself is known as the ***system unit***, and it contains many of the critical hardware and electrical components. The system unit is sometimes referred to as the tower, box, or console. When the system unit is combined with the appropriate peripheral devices, the system can perform the four basic computer functions: input, process, output, and storage. Peripheral devices are used to input and output data and information, and the system unit processes and stores the data.

System Unit

What is inside the system unit? If you remove the cover from the system unit, you will find several key components inside. One of the most essential components is the ***motherboard***, a large printed circuit board to which all the other components are connected (see Figure 1.7). The ***microprocessor chip***, also known as the ***central processing unit (CPU)*** and RAM, the computer's main memory, are connected to the motherboard (see the table in Figure 1.8). The motherboard also provides some of the ports used to connect peripheral devices to the system. Ports are explained and illustrated later in this chapter.

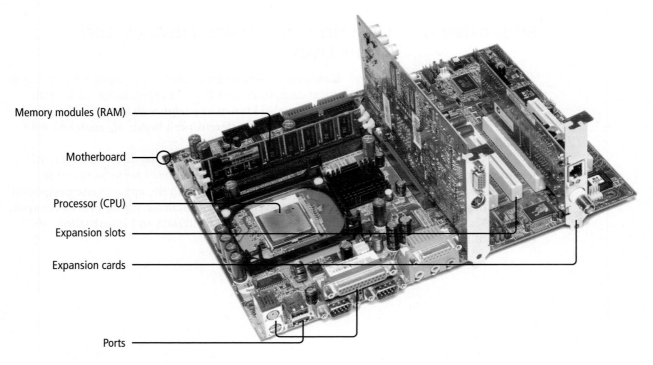

Memory modules (RAM)
Motherboard
Processor (CPU)
Expansion slots
Expansion cards
Ports

Figure 1.7
The motherboard and some of its components

Motherboard Features

Component	Description
Motherboard / System board	The main computer circuit board into which all components are plugged. It is installed safely inside the box or case called the system unit.
CPU	The central processing unit is responsible for getting data from memory, performing arithmetic and logical operations, and converting data to information.
Memory modules (RAM)	Temporary storage area where data is stored before processing, output, or storage. RAM is the center of flow of data and information within the information processing cycle.
Expansion slots	Slots or connectors on the motherboard that allow you to connect expansion cards.
Expansion cards	Removable circuit boards used to add new peripherals or increase the computer's capabilities. If the motherboard does not have a specific port to connect a peripheral device, the appropriate expansion card will allow you to do so.
Ports	Connecting points used as an interface between peripherals and the motherboard.

Figure 1.8
Motherboard features

Input Devices

Input devices are used to enter data into memory (RAM). The two most familiar input devices are the keyboard and the mouse, but they are not the only ones. See Figure 1.9.

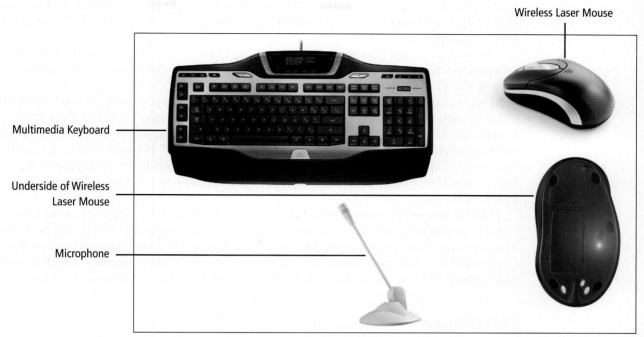

Wireless Laser Mouse

Multimedia Keyboard

Underside of Wireless Laser Mouse

Microphone

Figure 1.9
Input devices

Keyboards

Are there different types of keyboards? The **keyboard** is the primary input device for computers. There are actually several different kinds of keyboards. The QWERTY keyboard is the one most common. It is based on the original typewriter keyboard and is named for the arrangement of the letters on the upper left alphabetic row of keys. Another style is the Dvorak keyboard, which arranges the letters and numbers in a different pattern for increased typing speed. Some ergonomic keyboards use a split keyboard arrangement, offsetting each half at an angle to reduce the incidence of repetitive stress injuries such as carpal tunnel syndrome.

Keyboard size and layout on notebook and tablet computers can differ slightly from a standard keyboard due to space constraints. Keyboards usually send information to the computer through a cable connected to a USB port; however, **wireless** or remote keyboards are gaining in popularity. A wireless keyboard communicates with the computer by infrared or radio frequency technology. These wireless devices require batteries.

What are all these other keys used for? In addition to the standard alphanumeric keys originally found on typewriters, computer keyboards have a variety of keys that provide additional functionality.

Control keys, such as the Ctrl, Alt, and Windows keys, often provide shortcuts or increased functionality to the keyboard when used in combination with another key. If you press the Shift key and a letter, the result is an uppercase, rather than a lowercase, letter. In the same way, using one of the control keys enables the standard keys to be used for additional purposes. For example, pressing Ctrl and the letter P opens the Print dialog box. Another example of a control key is the Esc key, which can often be used to stop, or *escape*, from a currently running task. A unique control key that is found only on Windows-based keyboards is the Windows key.

The **numeric keypad**, located at the right of the keyboard, provides an alternative method of quickly entering numbers. This is useful for individuals who are accustomed to using an adding machine or calculator.

Function keys are located above the standard row of number keys. Numbered F1 through F12, these keys are generally associated with certain software-specific commands. Pressing the F1 key will usually open the Help menu for a program; however, pressing one of the other function keys can produce different results, depending on the software program running.

Arrow keys are the keys located at the bottom of the keyboard between the standard keys and the numeric keypad. These keys enable the user to move the insertion point around the window one space at a time.

Toggle and other keys, which are located just above the arrow keys, are used for various purposes, including navigation and editing. The Insert, Num Lock, and Caps Lock keys are all examples of toggle keys. A **toggle key** works just like a light switch; press it once and the feature is turned on, press it again and it is turned off. If you've ever accidentally pressed the Caps Lock key and typed a long string of all capital letters, you've seen this feature in action. Pressing the Caps Lock key again allows you to return to normal keyboarding mode.

Multimedia and Internet control keys are typically found at the top edge of the keyboard. The precise placement and function of these keys usually depends on the keyboard manufacturer. However, most modern keyboards have at least a few keys or buttons that can be used for such tasks as muting or adjusting speaker volume, opening a **Web browser**, and sending an e-mail. Generally, each button has an icon that indicates its function.

The Mouse

Is there an easier way to control the action on the computer screen? Yes, the **mouse** is an input device (also called a pointing device) that, together with the keyboard, enables the user to control the operations of the computer. The mouse became popular with the introduction of graphical user interfaces, such as Microsoft Windows. This point-and-click device is useful for positioning the **insertion point** by translating hand movements into corresponding actions on the screen. The mouse is represented on the screen by a symbol called the **mouse pointer**. The user can move the mouse and position this pointer anywhere on the screen to move objects or make selections from available program icons or menus.

Some mice have a roller ball on the bottom that, as you move it, translates your movement into electrical impulses. Others use laser technology (optical) to control the pointer movement. Because the bottom of an optical mouse is sealed, dirt and debris are less likely to get inside and interfere with the mouse's internal mechanisms. This laser beam can be harmful if pointed to your eyes; do not look at it directly or point it at anybody else's eyes. See Figure 1.4. Just like a keyboard, the mouse can be wired or wireless. Notebook and tablet computers can use a mouse, but most of them have a built-in touchpad, a trackball, or track point to move the insertion point and mouse pointer. Most mice today are equipped with two buttons and a wheel button in the center that provides easy zoom and scroll functions.

How can the mouse be used more efficiently? Although there are different kinds of mice, the traditional mouse has two buttons and a scroll wheel. The palm of your hand should rest comfortably over the mouse in such a way that your index finger rests on the left mouse button and the middle finger on the right mouse button. The following provides a brief description of some of the ways the mouse can be used:

- **Click**—By default, the left mouse button is considered the primary button. When instructed to click, it is understood that the mouse pointer is moved to a certain location on the screen and the left mouse button is be pressed and released one time.

- **Double-click**—When instructed to double-click, it is understood that the mouse pointer is moved to a certain location on the screen and the left mouse button is pressed and released twice in rapid succession. It is important that the mouse does not move while double-clicking or the command will not produce the expected results.

- **Drag**—This means to press the left mouse button and continue to hold it while dragging, or moving, the mouse then releasing it. This action can be used to select large blocks of text, to move objects, or to resize other objects.

- **Right-click**—Pressing and releasing the right mouse button one time will open a **shortcut menu**. Shortcut menus are usually context-sensitive, which means they will vary depending on what or where you have clicked and what program you are using. The right mouse button is also known as the secondary button and is not typically pressed more than one time; no double-clicking for the right button. After the shortcut menu has been opened, you select the appropriate choice by clicking it with the left mouse button.

- **Right-drag**—This is done by pressing the right mouse button and continuing to hold it while dragging, or moving, the mouse. This action is used when copying or moving files or folders within different storage devices.

- **Scroll wheel**—If your mouse is equipped with a scroll wheel, it can be used to quickly move a page up or down in a window, thus the name of the action to **scroll**. It is an easy way to navigate through lengthy documents or websites.

Are there other input devices? Although the keyboard and mouse are the two most common input devices, there are many other input devices. **Scanners** are similar to copy machines, but instead of producing a paper copy, they convert documents or photos to digital files that can then be saved on your computer. **Microphones** are used to digitally capture and record sounds. Game controls such as **joysticks** are used to control movement within video games. **Digital cameras** and **digital video recorders** enable you to capture digital images and movies and transfer them directly to your computer.

The Processor

What does the CPU do? The CPU (see Figure 1.10) is the brain of the computer and is responsible for executing program instructions and manipulating data to convert to information. It has two main parts—the ***control unit*** and the ***arithmetic logic unit (ALU).*** The control unit is responsible for obtaining and executing instructions from the computer's memory. Example: The user wants to print a document and selects the "Print" command from an icon on the screen. The CPU gets the command from memory (RAM), interprets the command, and sends the document as output to a selected printer. In other words, the CPU coordinates the internal activities and the activities of all the other computer components. The arithmetic logic unit (ALU) performs the arithmetic and logic functions for the computer. The ALU handles addition, subtraction, multiplication, and division, and also makes logical and comparison decisions. This enables the CPU to perform tasks such as sorting data alphabetically or numerically and filtering data to locate specific criteria.

Figure 1.10
Two sides of a CPU

Different CPUs

As important as the CPU is to your computer, you might expect it to take up a large amount of space in the console. However, the CPU is actually rather small, thus the term *microchip.* Over the years, manufacturers have successfully reduced the size of microprocessor chips while continuing to increase their computing power. In fact, Moore's law (formulated in 1965 by Gordon Moore, cofounder of Intel) addresses this increase in computing power, observing that current production methods enable CPU capacity to double about every 24 months or so!

Are there different brands of CPUs? Yes, the most well-known chip manufacturers include Intel and Advanced Micro Devices (AMD). Chip manufacturers often produce several different models of chips. Some of the chips that Intel makes include the *Intel® Core™ i7 processor Extreme Edition,* the *Intel® Core™2 Quad Processor* for desktops, and the *Intel® Centrino® 2 Processor Technology* for portable computers. AMD manufactures chips such as the *AMD Phenom™ II X4* for desktops, and the *AMD Turion™ X2 Ultra Dual-Core Mobile Processor* for portable computers. Intel and AMD chips are the mainstays for PCs. Using multiple processors (dual core or quad core) has several advantages over a single-processor CPU, including improved multitasking capabilities and system performance, lower power consumption, reduced usage of system resources, and lower heat emissions.

How is a CPU's processing power measured? One indicator of a CPU's processing power is its ***clock speed.*** Clock speed measures the speed at which a CPU processes data (number of instructions per second) and is measured in ***megahertz (MHz)*** or ***gigahertz***

(GHz), depending on the age of the CPU. Early computers had CPUs that processed at speeds of less than 5 MHz, whereas modern processors can operate at over 3 GHz (the equivalent of 3,000 MHz) and newer processors continue to surpass these numbers.

What types of memory does a computer have? Memory is another critical computer component of a computer system. The term *memory* signifies storage. There are two basic types of memory: temporary or ***volatile*** and permanent or ***nonvolatile.***

Permanent memory includes ***Read-Only Memory (ROM),*** which is prerecorded on a chip. The information on a ROM chip cannot be changed, removed, or rewritten, and is generally inaccessible to the computer user. ROM is nonvolatile memory because it retains its contents even if the computer is turned off. ROM contains critical information, such as the program used to start up or boot—start— the computer.

Storage devices such as hard disks and flash drives and storage media such as CDs and DVDs are considered permanent or nonvolatile memory. These are presented later in this chapter.

Temporary memory, the computer's temporary or volatile memory, is ***Random Access Memory (RAM)***. RAM (see Figure 1.11) acts as the computer's short-term memory and stores data and program instructions waiting to be processed. RAM is considered volatile because its contents are erased when the computer is turned off.

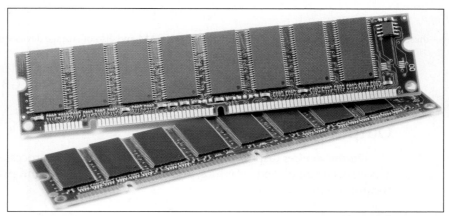

Figure 1.11
Random Access Memory (RAM) / RAM chips

Why is it important to have enough RAM? The more tasks your computer performs at the same time, or the more programs you have open, the more RAM it uses. We described RAM earlier as the center of the flow of data and information in the information processing cycle (see Figure 1.1). That flow slows down when there is not enough RAM. Your computer's RAM is like the top of your desk. The size of the desk that you need is determined by the work you do at a given moment. You may need to use a notebook computer, several books, a clipboard with notes, a holder for pens and pencils, and a telephone. If your desk is not big enough to fit these items, you cannot work with all of them at the same time. If you do not have a sufficient amount of RAM in your system, you might notice your computer slows down or even stops responding when you try to perform tasks.

Computer users often think this means they have too much information saved on their computers' hard drives. What it actually means is that they are running out of memory, not permanent storage space. To fix this problem, you can reduce the number of programs running at the same time, disable some features of the Operating System, or simply add more RAM to your system. Installing additional memory is one of the most inexpensive and easiest upgrades for your computer and often results in noticeable performance improvements.

Memory is measured in several units such as ***megabytes (MB)***, which is approximately one million bytes, ***gigabytes (GB)***, which is approximately one billion bytes, or ***terabytes (TR)***, which is one trillion bytes. Study the table in Figure 1.12.

Units to Measure Memory

Name	Abbreviation	Number of Bytes	Relative Size
Byte	**B**	1 byte	Holds one character of data
Kilobyte	**KB**	1,024 bytes	Holds about a half page of double-spaced text
Megabyte	**MB**	1,048,576 bytes	Holds about 768 pages of typed text
Gigabyte	**GB**	1,073,741,824 bytes	Holds approximately 786,432 pages of text
Terabyte	**TB**	1,099,511,627,776 bytes	This represents a stack of typewritten pages almost 51 miles high
Petabyte	**PB**	1,125,899,906,842,624 bytes	This represents a stack of typewritten pages almost 52,000 miles high

Figure 1.12

Measuring memory—these units are used to measure the size and capacity of RAM and also of storage devices/media

RAM size requirements vary depending on the operating system in use. Older computers that run Windows XP should have between 512 MB to 1 GB of RAM. For newer computers, a minimum of 2GB possibly more is recommended.

Output Devices

Output devices display information after data has been processed in a useful format. This format can be text, graphics, audio, or video. Monitors and printers are the two most common output devices.

Monitors

What are monitors? Monitors are display devices that show images of text, graphics, and video once data has been processed. The image on a monitor is called ***soft copy***; you can view it, but you cannot touch it. See Figure 1.13.

Touch screen display   LCD Wide monitor

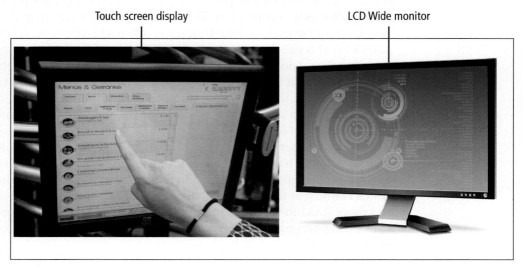

Figure 1.13

Output devices—monitors

What is an LCD monitor? Monitors come in a variety of sizes and styles, but the standard today is the ***LCD (liquid crystal display)***. ***Flat-panel*** LCD monitors use a liquid crystal display and are thin and energy efficient.

What factors determine a monitor's display quality? The number of ***pixels***, a monitor's display, is made up of millions of tiny dots known as pixels or picture element. Each pixel represents a single point on a display screen or in a graphic image. The number of pixels on the screen determines a monitor's sharpness and clarity, also known as its ***resolution***. A higher number of pixels results in a clearer and sharper monitor resolution. A standard screen resolution might be expressed as 1024 x 768, which means there are 1,024 columns, each containing 768 pixels, for a total of more than 786,000 pixels on the screen. Monitor sizes are determined by measuring their screens diagonally.

Dot pitch is another display characteristic and refers to the diagonal distance between two pixels of the same color. Dot pitch is measured in millimeters with smaller measurements resulting in a crisper viewing image because there is less blank space between the pixels. For best viewing, monitors should have a dot pitch measurement of .28 mm or less. LCD monitors use an electric current to illuminate the pixels.

Refresh rate is the speed at which the pixels are reilluminated and it's measured in cycles per second, expressed as hertz (Hz). Refresh rates generally average between 75 and 85 Hz, which means the screen image is redrawn 75 to 85 times per second. Higher refresh rates result in less screen flicker and less eye strain.

What are touch screen monitors? Touch screen monitors are both input and output devices. They display images just like regular monitors but also enable users to touch their surfaces and make selections directly from the screen. These monitors are widely used in retail stores at checkout counters, in airports for passengers' fast check-ins, and HP has released a personal computer in which the monitor is also the system unit and uses touch screen technology.

Which monitor is best? Choosing the right monitor is always a combination of what you like, want, and can afford. A higher resolution, small dot pitch, fast refresh rate, and large monitor size are desirable, but all come with a higher price tag.

Printers

Using a monitor is a good way to view the information on your computer, but sometimes a soft copy isn't sufficient for your needs. **Printers** generate a **hard copies** or **printouts**, which are a permanent record of your work on paper. See Figure 1.14.

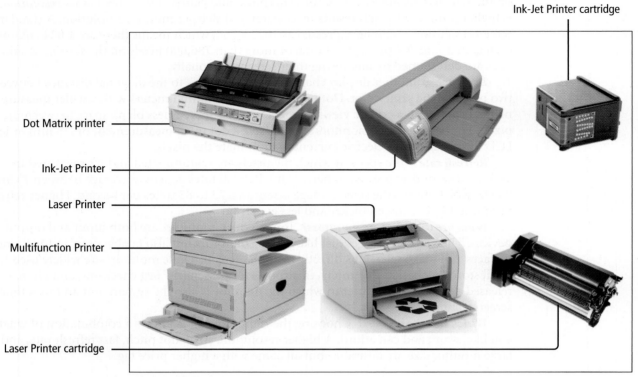

Figure 1.14
Output devices—printers

What types of printers are available? There are two categories of printers: impact and nonimpact. **Impact** printers have small hammers, similar to a typewriter's, that strike an ink ribbon against paper, leaving behind the image of the character or symbol. The **dot matrix** printer is an impact printer. Once very popular because of their low cost, dot matrix printers are still in use today, limited only to certain applications that require continuous forms or multipart forms (an original and several copies), such as invoices or purchase orders.

How does a nonimpact printer work? **Nonimpact** printers do not actually touch the paper when printing. There are a variety of nonimpact printers, but the two most commonly used with home computers are the ink-jet printer and the laser printer. The **ink-jet** printer uses a special nozzle and ink cartridges to spray ink in small droplets onto the surface of the paper. Ink-jet printers easily print in color, in black, and in grayscale to produce good quality printouts. They are relatively inexpensive to buy and maintain. **Laser printers** use the same process as photocopiers to produce their output. They use a special cylinder known as a drum, dry ink or toner, and a laser. Static electricity attracts toner to the surface of the drum, and the laser distributes the toner in the correct pattern. The drum transfers the toner to the paper and heat is used to permanently fuse the toner to the paper. Laser printers are generally more expensive to purchase than ink-jet printers, although they often print more quickly and are more cost effective. Lower-end laser printers print only in black and white; however, more expensive printers can produce color copies.

How do you assess a printer's capabilities? When you select a printer, there are some key characteristics to consider.

Print speed is often expressed as ***pages per minute (ppm)***. Print speed can vary depending on the manufacturer and model, and is also affected by whether the page is text-only, if it includes graphics, and if the printout is in color or in black and grayscale.

Just as with monitors, resolution is also important to print quality. For printing purposes, resolution is expressed as ***dots per inch*** or ***dpi***. The higher the dpi, the better the print quality. Print qualities of 300 to 600 dpi are typical of most printers, although special photo printers can offer resolutions up to 1,200 dpi. Professional printers can reach even higher values.

Color output and its related cost is another important consideration. Ink-jet printers offer four- or six-color options. Many ink-jet printers use one cartridge for black ink and one or more cartridges for color. When available, printers that offer a separate cartridge for each color are a practical choice because you need to replace only one color at a time as the cartridges run out. Laser printers use separate toner cartridges for each color.

What are all-in-one printers? All-in-one printers bundle multiple capabilities in one device. All-in-one devices usually include:

- A printer, either ink-jet (color or black and grayscale) or laser (output)

- A scanner to convert text or images into files that can be stored and further manipulated by the computer (input)

- A facsimile (fax) function to send and receive documents via the telephone (communications)

- A copier function to duplicate documents (output)

- Network capabilities to enable this ***multifunction device (MFD)*** to work as part of a network environment both wired or wireless (communications)

Speakers and Multimedia Projectors

Are there other output devices? ***Speakers*** and ***multimedia projectors*** are also examples of output devices. Many computers include small speakers to enable the user to listen to CDs or DVDs and hear any auditory signals the computer sends. However, if you're serious about multimedia, you will probably want to invest in a better set of speakers for improved performance. Multimedia projectors are used to conduct presentations and training sessions. These projectors enable information to be displayed on a big screen so it can be easily viewed by a large group of attendees.

Under what category do digital cameras fall? A digital camera is a device that stores pictures digitally rather than using conventional film. After images are captured, they are stored in the camera's internal memory. Some cameras use removable flash memory cards as storage media. These cards can be read by a computer, which can then edit them and save them as files. So, the camera itself is a form of "hand-held" computer, which, if connected to a computer, serves as an input/output device. The same thing can be said to describe camcorders.

Storage Devices

What are storage devices? **Storage devices** are used to store the data, information, and programs for future use. This storage is often referred to as permanent memory because, unlike data that is in RAM, data saved to a storage device remains there until the user deletes or overwrites it. Data can be stored using internal hardware devices located in the system unit or in removable units that enable portability. See Figure 1.15.

Figure 1.15
Storage devices

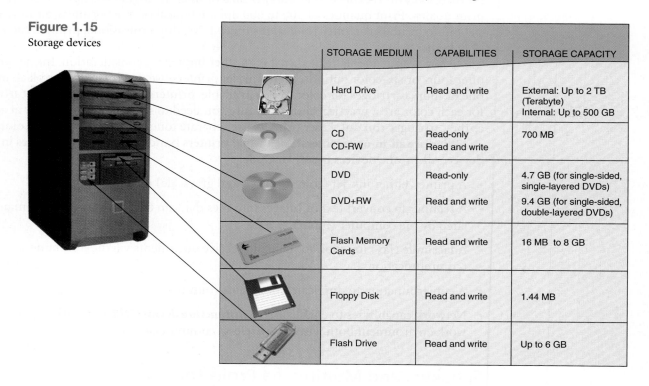

STORAGE MEDIUM	CAPABILITIES	STORAGE CAPACITY
Hard Drive	Read and write	External: Up to 2 TB (Terabyte) Internal: Up to 500 GB
CD CD-RW	Read-only Read and write	700 MB
DVD	Read-only	4.7 GB (for single-sided, single-layered DVDs)
DVD+RW	Read and write	9.4 GB (for single-sided, double-layered DVDs)
Flash Memory Cards	Read and write	16 MB to 8 GB
Floppy Disk	Read and write	1.44 MB
Flash Drive	Read and write	Up to 6 GB

How is a storage device different than storage media? A **device** is a piece of hardware such as a hard drive or a DVD drive. Media is the removable part that actually contains the stored data. Media requires a device to **read** and **write** on it. Read is the action of retrieving or opening existing data and write is the action of saving or storing data. Following is a list of devices and their media:

- CD and DVD optical drives read and write on CDs and DVDs, which are the media.

- Card readers read and write on flash memory cards, which are the media.

- Flash drives or thumb drives are media that require a connection to a USB port for read/write operations.

- Tape backup drives read and write onto tape cartridges, which are the media.

- The exception to this is the hard drive, in which the hardware and the media are all contained in a sealed unit that cannot be taken apart.

How is data stored? Data is generally stored using one of three forms of storage: magnetic, optical, or flash memory:

- **Magnetic** storage uses tape or film covered in a thin, magnetic coating that enables data to be saved as magnetic impulses. It works in much the same fashion as an audiocassette or videotape works. Hard drives and backup tape drives are both forms of magnetic storage. Before magnetic storage can occur, media has to be formatted. This is the process in which media is divided into *tracks* and *sectors*. Tracks are magnetic concentric circles and sectors are segments within those circles Data is stored magnetically within the spaces created by these tracks sectors. Magnetic media has read/write capability, which means it is possible to use it over and over again, enabling you to delete or revise existing data and save new data.

- ***Optical*** storage uses flat plastic discs coated in a special reflective material. Data is saved by using a laser beam to burn tiny pits into the storage medium. A less intensive laser is used to read the saved data. The saved data is organized using tracks and sectors, similar to those used in magnetic media. ***Compact discs (CDs)*** and ***digital video discs (DVDs)*** are examples of optical media. Unlike magnetic media, not all optical storage is read/write capable. ***CD-ROMs***—CD media that was burned once and from that moment on can only be read—and ***DVD-ROMs***—DVD media that is burned once and from that moment on can only be read—are considered read-only media (ROM). The information contained on them can be read, but not changed or deleted, and it is not possible to save new data to them. If you purchase new software, music, or a movie, it is most likely on a CD-ROM or DVD-ROM. A record-only disc (CD-R) enables you to record, or ***burn***, information to the disc one time only; information saved this way cannot be deleted or rewritten. A rewritable disc (CD-RW) enables information to be recorded, revised, or deleted, and new data can also be written to the disc, similar to magnetic media. The same possibilities are available in DVDs. However, there are currently two competing formats DVD-R/RW, known as "DVD dash," and DVD+R/RW, known as "DVD plus." The R/RW suffix indicates the DVD can be used to record and can also be rewritten. Although most DVD players can play either format, if you want to record to a DVD, you need to know which format the DVD recorder requires.

What is LightScribe? **LightScribe** is a disc-labeling technology that burns text and graphics onto the surface of a specially coated LightScribe CD or DVD. This is an alternative to printing a conventional sticker label and attaching it to a regular CD or DVD but it does require that you purchase LightScribe media. See Figure 1.16.

Figure 1.16
LightScribe direct disc labeling

- **Flash memory** uses solid-state technology. It is completely electronic and has no moving mechanical parts. Flash memory is a quick and easy form of rewritable storage and is often used in mobile devices such as PDAs, digital cameras, and MP3 players. Depending on the manufacturer, flash memory cards may be called Memory Stick, CompactFlash, Secure Digital, or MultiMediaCard. Typically, a device can use only one style of memory card; however, a computer equipped with the appropriate card reader can read any of them. Small, removable storage devices known as flash drives or thumb drives also use flash technology, require a USB port to connect to the system unit, and are very popular to transport data.

What are the main types of storage devices? Depending on the age and type of computer you have, you might find some or all of the following internal storage options:

- **Hard disk drive**—A hard disk drive is the computer's main internal storage device. Also referred to as a hard drive, its storage space is usually measured in gigabytes (GB), with newer computers ranging in size from 80 GB to 750 GB, although it is possible to find some specialized, high-end computers with storage space measuring up to 2 terabytes (TB). As with everything else in computing, these numbers tend to increase with each new model. Hard drives are traditionally permanent storage devices fixed inside the system unit.

- **Floppy disk drive**—This is a device that reads/writes floppy diskettes that have a maximum storage capacity of 1,450 MB. Because of this limited storage capacity compared to other media, you will seldom see floppy disks used by computer users today.

- **CD and/or DVD drives**—Your computer may have one or two of these optical drives in the system unit. It's important to know whether these drives are simple CD-ROM drives, which can only read CDs, or if it is a **CD-RW** drive, also known as a CD burner. A **CD burner** gives you the ability to save, or burn, files to a CD-R (compact disk recordable). You might also have a separate drive that can read and/or write DVDs.

Although CDs and DVDs look alike, DVDs are capable of holding much more information than CDs. A CD can hold up to 700 MB of data, but a DVD can store almost 10 GB! Because of their differences, a CD drive is unable to read DVDs, although a DVD drive can read CDs.

Is it possible to add a storage device to a system? If you are running out of hard disk space or your system doesn't have a particular storage device, it may be possible to add a storage device, provided your system has enough room for it. You would need an available drive bay, which is the physical location within the system unit, or you might consider removing an existing device and replacing it with another. For instance, if you only have a CD-ROM drive, you could remove that and replace it with a CD-RW/DVD drive, thereby giving you the ability to read and burn CDs and play DVDs too. It is also possible to purchase many of these units as external storage devices. An external storage device is a peripheral that attaches to the computer via a port and performs the same tasks as its corresponding internal device. One of the most popular of these today is the external hard drive, which can greatly increase a computer's storage capacity and make your data fully portable.

Are there other types of storage devices? Other storage devices you might be familiar with include flash drives, a currently popular form of data storage, and older but still reliable backup tape drives.

Flash drives are removable storage devices that use flash memory and connect to the computer by a USB port. Flash drives are also known as thumb drives, universal serial bus (USB) drives, and jump drives. The flash drive is typically a device small enough to fit on a keychain or in a pocket and, because of its solid-state circuitry and lack of moving parts, it is extremely durable. Available in several storage sizes ranging from 16 MB to 64 GB, a flash drive is a quick and easy way to save and transport files. As an example, a 64-MB flash drive, which is relatively small, holds the equivalent of almost 45 floppy disks! To use one of these devices, you simply plug it into a computer's USB port. The computer recognizes the new device and enables the user to save or retrieve files from the flash drive.

Backup tape drives are storage devices that resemble audiocassette tape recorders and save data to magnetic tape media. Although they are rarely used for home computers anymore, many businesses and organizations still rely on tape backup systems to safeguard their data on a daily basis. See Figure 1.17.

The capacity of the components found in your system unit is measured in terms of storage size or speed. Computer systems continue to increase in storage capacity and

Figure 1.17
Tape backup drive and media

computing speed, while decreasing in size. Generally, higher measurements indicate a system that is quicker and more powerful than a system with lower measurements. However, it is important to balance size and speed with financial considerations too. Although it is tempting to consider buying a computer with the most power possible, a lesser computer may be more reasonably priced and still be sufficient for the typical user's needs. Recall that CPU speed is measured in megahertz (MHz) or gigahertz (GHz). The amount of RAM in a computer is generally measured in megabytes (MB), while storage space is usually measured in megabytes or gigabytes (GB), depending on the device.

Ports

What are ports? A **port** acts as an interface or connector between a system's peripheral devices and the computer, enabling data to be exchanged easily. Ports (see Figure 1.18) have different shapes and sizes. The same ports are typically found on a desktop too, although they might be arranged in a different order. Various input and output devices use different data exchange methods, requiring different types of ports and connectors (or plugs). If your computer does not have a particular port, you can buy an expansion card that connects to the motherboard and provides the needed connection.

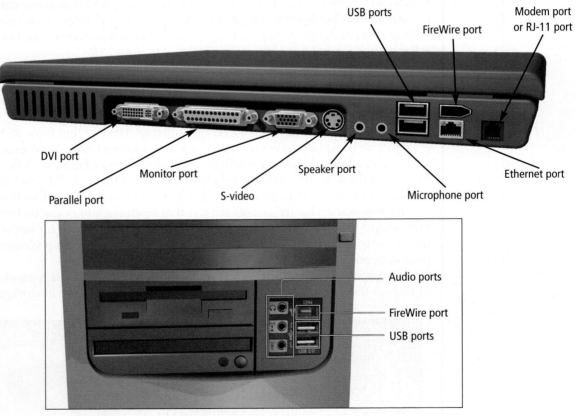

Figure 1.18
Ports

How do you determine which port a peripheral device needs? Manufacturers have attempted to make the process of connecting peripheral devices less complicated on newer computers. Rather than trying to match the size and shape of a connector to its port, many manufacturers now use a color-coding system that coordinates the colors of the connectors with their corresponding ports. Additionally, many newer desktop computers include ports, such as USB and audio ports, on the front panel of the system unit to provide easier access to them. Locating these ports on the front or back panels makes it a simple process to connect and disconnect devices that are used only occasionally, such as digital cameras, external hard drives, or MP3 players. Peripherals that are rarely disconnected, such as a keyboard or printer, are generally plugged into the ports on the back of the computer.

What are the different ports used for? Serial and parallel ports are two of the oldest types of ports found on a computer. *Serial ports* are ports that can send data only one bit at a time, so the data exchange rate is slow compared to newer technology. The maximum rate at which a standard serial port can transfer data is 115 *kilobits* or one thousand bits per second (Kbps). The mouse and modem are examples of devices that might use a serial port. A *parallel port* is a port that sends data in groups of bits, at transfer rates of up to 500 Kbps, so it is a considerably faster method of transferring data than the serial port. Older printers were often connected to a computer through a parallel port.

Are there faster ports? Over the years, newer ports have come into existence. One of these is the *universal serial bus (USB) port*. This type of port is able to interface with several different peripheral devices, which reduces the need for individual, dedicated ports. USB ports are also able to transfer data at extremely high rates of speed. Original USB ports, known as USB 1.1, are capable of speeds of 12 *megabits* or one million bits per second (Mbps). The newest version, USB 2.0, can attain a rate of 480 Mbps, 40 times faster than USB 1.1 technology and over 400 times faster than a serial port! USB 2.0 ports are backwards compatible, which means that older USB devices work with them; however, data will transfer only at the slower USB 1.1 speed. The higher data transfer capabilities of USB ports, coupled with their capability to work with multiple devices, have made the older serial and parallel ports obsolete. Because of the USB port's speedy data transfer rate and its capability to be used with numerous devices, new computers often include six or more USB ports. Devices using USB ports include keyboards, mice, printers, scanners, digital cameras, MP3 players, and PDAs. In general, it's a good idea to get a computer with as many USB ports as possible. See the table in Figure 1.19.

Ports and Their Uses

Port Name	Data Transfer Speed	Typical Use
Serial	115 Kbps	Mice / External modems
Parallel	500 Kbps	Printers / External Zip drives
USB 1.1	12 Mbps	Mice / Keyboards / Printers / Scanners / Game controllers
USB 2.0	400 Mbps	Same as USB 1.1 but at faster transfer rates. Also, camcorders, digital cameras, and MP3 players. It maintains compatibility with USB 1.1.
FireWire / FireWire 800	400 Mbps / 800 Mbps	Digital video camcorders / Digital cameras
Ethernet / Gigabit Ethernet	Up to 100 Mbps / Up to 1,000 Mbps	Network connections / Cable modems

Figure 1.19
Port speeds and uses

The *FireWire port*, developed by Apple and also known as IEEE 1394, is another means of transferring data quickly. The FireWire 400 has a data transfer rate of 400 Mbps, while the newer FireWire 800 transfers data at a blazing 800 Mbps! This port is typically used to connect devices that need to transfer huge amounts of data to a computer quickly, such as digital cameras or digital video recorders, or external hard drives. FireWire ports are standard on many Apple products, but are usually found only on higher-end Windows PCs and peripheral devices. Some peripheral devices offer users a choice of connecting using a USB port or a FireWire port.

What kind of port is used to connect to another computer? Connectivity ports, such as Ethernet and modem ports, are used to connect a computer to a local network or to the Internet. An ***Ethernet port***, also known as an RJ-45 jack, resembles a standard phone jack, but is slightly larger. The Ethernet port is used for network access and can also be used to connect a cable modem or router for Internet access. A ***modem port*** is the same size and shape as a phone jack and is used to connect the modem to a phone system, enabling ***digital subscriber line (DSL)*** or dial-up Internet access. DSL is a type of communications line in which signals travel through copper wires between a telephone switching station and a home or business. The maximum data transfer rate for a modem is 56 Kbps, whereas the most common Ethernet standard, Fast Ethernet, transfers data at the rate of 100 Mbps. However, Gigabit Ethernet, with a potential transfer rate of 1,000 Mbps, is becoming an option on higher-end systems and is standard on many Mac systems.

Even faster Ethernet technologies, such as 10 Gigabit Ethernet or 10 GbE exist, but they are currently used for network backbones and enterprise network infrastructures rather than home users.

Are there special purpose ports? Despite the prevalence of USB ports, which can be used for a variety of peripherals, there are still some devices that require special ports. These ports include Musical Instrument Digital Interface (MIDI), IrDA, Bluetooth, video, and audio ports.

MIDI ports are used to connect electronic musical devices, such as keyboards and synthesizers, to a computer, enabling musicians to create digital music files.

The ***IrDA port*** is used to enable devices such as PDAs, keyboards, mice, and printers to transmit data wirelessly to another device by using infrared light waves. In order to transmit information, each of the devices must have an IrDA port, and a clear line of sight, with no other objects blocking the transmission.

Bluetooth is another type of wireless technology that relies on radio wave transmission and doesn't require a clear line of sight. Bluetooth-enabled devices such as PDAs or other mobile devices can communicate only with each other over short distances, typically less than 30 feet.

Video ports include standard monitor ports, DVI ports, and S-video ports. A ***monitor port*** is used to connect the monitor to the graphics processing unit, which is usually located on the motherboard or on a video card. However, to get the best results from a flat-panel (LCD) monitor, the ***Digital Video Interface (DVI) port*** should be used instead. The DVI port transmits a pure digital signal, eliminating the need for digital-to-analog conversion and resulting in a higher quality transmission and a clearer picture on the monitor. The ***S-video port*** is typically used to connect other video sources, such as a television, projector, or digital recorder, to the computer.

Similar to video ports, ***audio ports*** connect audio devices, such as speakers, headphones, and microphones, to the computer's sound card. These jacks will be familiar to anyone who is used to using standard stereo components.

Evaluating Your System

Each computer might have a different configuration. The way a computer system is set up or the combination of components that make up the system is called its ***configuration***. This is important when buying a computer, expanding an existing system, or when connecting computers together in a network environment.

Now that you have learned most of the hardware components of a typical personal computer, you are ready to explore the computer's configuration, specifications, and features. If you didn't buy your computer brand new, you might not know all the details about your computer. If you did buy a new computer, the easiest way is to check your paperwork; all the basic information should be there. However, if your computer isn't new or you didn't keep the paperwork, there are some ways to determine exactly what is in your system. Also if you start a new job or a new position and are given a computer system, you can do a number of things again to determine exactly what is in your system.

What kind of computer do you have? This is one of the easiest questions to answer. Like almost every other appliance you've used, you can probably find the manufacturer's name and a brand name or model number on the case of the computer. If not, check the back of the unit; there should be a metal tag that includes the manufacturer's name, model number, and serial number. This information might be necessary if you have to have service performed under warranty. Use the following steps to see your system properties, which will answer some questions.

If you are a Windows XP user and you have the My Computer icon on the desktop:

1 Right-click My Computer.

2 Select Properties and read the contents of the General tab.

If you do not have the My Computer icon on the desktop, follow these steps:

1 Click the **Start** menu, select **Settings**, and then click **Control Panel**.

2 From the next window, click **Performance** and **Maintenance**.

3 Then click **System** and read the contents of the **General** tab.

Windows Vista users can follow these steps:

1 Right-click the **My Computer** icon on the desktop and select **Properties**.

2 If the icon is not on the desktop, open the **Start** menu and then right-click the **Computer** button and select **Properties**. See Figure 1.20.

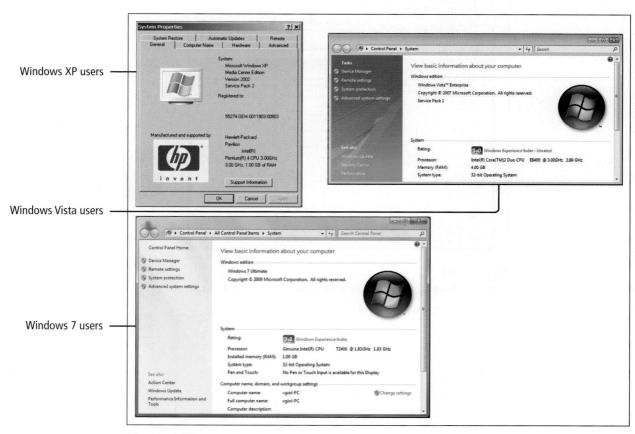

Figure 1.20
Evaluating your system—General Properties

What operating system does the computer use? If you watch carefully as a computer boots up, you can often determine the operating system. You will usually see a ***splash screen*** showing the version of Windows that runs—for example, Windows ME, Windows XP, Windows Vista, or Windows 7, which is the working name for a new version of Windows to be released sometime in 2010.

How much memory is in the computer? What is the type and speed of the CPU? Figure 1.21 displays (for several versions of Windows) a window with information on the computer's operating system, the type and speed of the CPU, and the storage capacity of RAM.

How do you determine what drives are on the system and how much storage space is available? It's important to know how much information you can store on your computer, what disk drives are available, and how much room you have left on each drive. Is there enough storage space or are the storage devices getting full? Use My Computer (or Computer) to find the answers. If the desktop does not have a My Computer (or Computer) icon, you can access it through the Start menu.

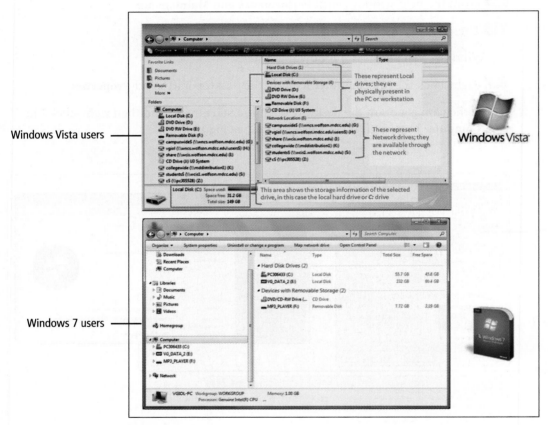

Figure 1.21
Using Windows Explorer to view the drives available to your computer

Figure 1.22 shows the Computer (or Windows Explorer) window in which the user can see all available local drives (devices within the system unit or peripherals to that unit) and network drives (devices available through a network). Also, right-click on any drive symbol, and select Properties from the shortcut menu. A new dialog box displays the drive's information similar to the one shown in Figure 1.22. The pie chart displayed on the General tab is a good visual tool that shows the size of your storage device and how much space is free.

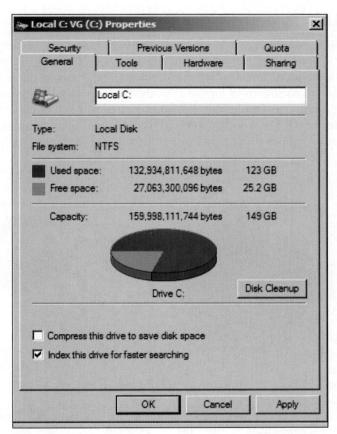

Figure 1.22
The properties of one of the storage drives (the hard drive)

Objective 4 | Identify Types of Software and Their Uses

So far we have described computer hardware, the physical components of the system. However, without software, the computer would just be a collection of useless electronic and mechanical parts. Software provides the instructions or commands that tell the computer what to do. To perform various tasks, the computer requires a set of instructions called **programs**. These programs enable individuals to use the computer without the need for special programming skills. There are two categories of computer software—**system software** and **application software**. Both types of software are required to work effectively with your computer.

System Software

System software provides the instructions that the computer needs to run. It contains the directions needed to start up the computer (known as the **boot process**), checks to ensure everything is in good working order, and enables you to interface or interact with the computer and its peripheral devices so that you can use them. System software consists of two main programs: the **operating system** and **utility programs**.

Operating Systems

What is the operating system? The **operating system (OS)** is a special computer program that is present on every desktop computer, notebook, PDAs, or mainframes. The operating system controls the way the computer works from the time it is turned on until it is shut down. As shown in Figure 1.23, the operating system manages the various hardware components, including the CPU, memory, storage devices, peripheral devices, and network devices. It also coordinates with the various software applications presently running and provides the interaction with the user (user interface).

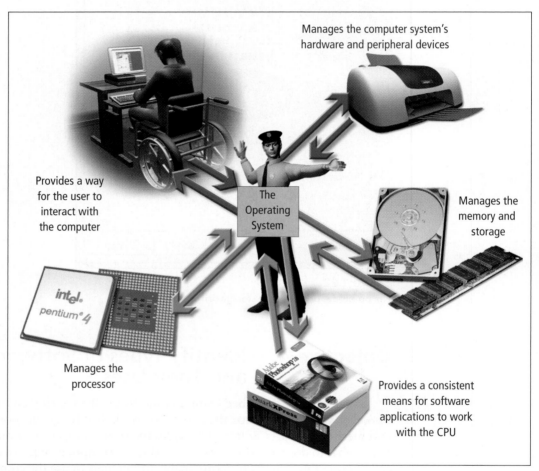

Manages the computer system's hardware and peripheral devices

Provides a way for the user to interact with the computer

The Operating System

Manages the memory and storage

Manages the processor

Provides a consistent means for software applications to work with the CPU

Figure 1.23
The operating system

Is it possible to communicate with the operating system? Although the operating system communicates with the computer and its peripherals, it also includes a **user interface** that you can use to interact and communicate with the computer. Early operating systems used a text-based or keyboard-driven interface. The early **Disk Operating System (DOS)** required knowledge of special commands that had to be typed accurately to achieve the desired results. This type of system was not very "**user friendly.**" Most current operating systems use a point-and-click format known as a *graphical user interface (GUI)*. GUIs are more user friendly and intuitive than DOS systems. Rather than typing specific commands, you can use a mouse to select from on screen objects such as *icons* (a graphical depiction of an object such as a file or program), *menus* (lists of available commands), or *dialog boxes* (windows used to make choices or give the system specific instructions as to the action you want to take or task to perform). GUI operating systems display information on the monitor in the form of rectangular boxes called *windows*. Although you interact with system software every time you use the computer, in some ways you don't notice it.

Do all computers need an operating system? Yes, the operating system is a critical part of a computer system. Without an OS to provide specific instructions, the computer would be unable to fulfill its four main functions. However, different computers require different types of operating systems. There are several popular operating systems available for home computers. They include Microsoft Windows, Mac OS, and Linux.

Microsoft Windows has the largest market share of the three main operating systems and is found on most of today's desktop and notebook computers. There have been many versions of Microsoft Windows, including Windows 3.0, Windows 95, Windows 98, Windows Me, Windows Vista, and Windows 7 to be released in 2010. Although a previous version of Windows might be found on an older computer, Windows Vista is the current version installed on most computers. A sample Windows Vista desktop is displayed in Figure 1.24.

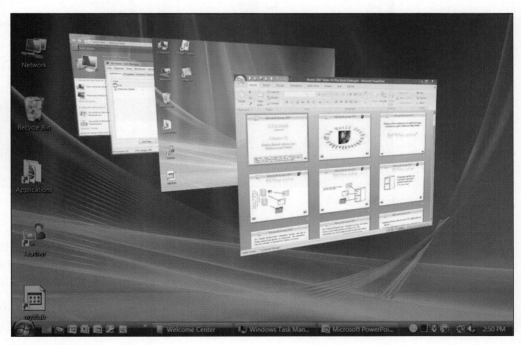

Figure 1.24
A sample of the Windows VISTA desktop

Why are there so many versions of Windows? Software developers are always updating and refining their software to adapt to new technology, respond to vulnerabilities, and improve their product. Because Microsoft also manufactures application software, some of its products have similar names and users can become confused. It's important to note that even though your computer might use Microsoft Windows for its operating system, it might not have Microsoft Office (an application software suite) installed.

Mac OS is an operating system designed specifically for Apple's Macintosh computers. Figure 1.25 shows the Mac OS desktop that is similar to Windows because it also uses a GUI. In fact, Apple was the first company to introduce a commercially successful GUI operating system for the consumer market. But, because of the popularity of the Windows-based PCs, Mac OS has a much smaller market share. If you are looking to purchase a PC or a peripheral for a PC, you have a variety of choices among different manufacturers. Only Apple manufactures Apple products and peripherals for its computers and they tend to be a bit pricier.

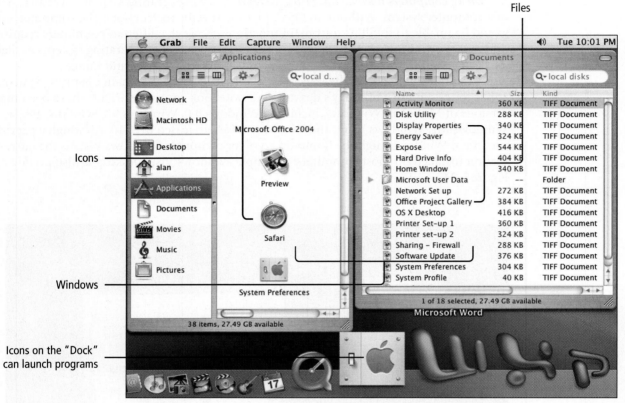

Figure 1.25
Mac OS desktop

Can Windows run on an Apple computer? Until recently, the Mac OS could not run on a PC, and the Windows OS could not run on a Mac. Software is available to start a Mac that will run Windows applications. Microsoft's Virtual PC for Mac features specifications such as:

• Access PC-only software, files, networks, and devices with your Mac

• Zero-configuration printing; better graphics handling; expanded preferences

• Cut and paste between platforms; share folders and other media between platforms

• Easily shut down virtual PC and relaunch right where it left off

• Use PC and Mac peripherals

Linux is an alternative operating system. Based on the UNIX operating system developed for mainframe computers, it also has a dedicated group of users. Linux is an **open-source** operating system, which means it is not owned by a single company and some versions are available at no cost.

How is open-source software different from other types of software? Open-source software makes its source code, essentially the program instructions, available to anyone who would like to see it. Programmers are encouraged to work with and change the code as they see fit, in the hope that having many "eyes" looking at the code will streamline and improve it. Proprietary software, such as Microsoft Windows, keeps this code secret and inaccessible to programmers who are not authorized by the software development company.

Why is Linux used? Linux is rarely used by novice computer users, although it is popular among developers and other technologically advanced individuals who prefer to use an alternative operating system. Some people appreciate the opportunity to work in this more "open" programming environment. However, one of the disadvantages of Linux is that, because no single company is responsible for it, technical support is not easily found. Users might find help from various resources such as user groups and Internet communities. Alternatively, some software companies have chosen to develop and sell a version of Linux that includes a warranty and technical support as a way of alleviating user concerns. Figure 1.26 shows an example of one version of the Linux operating system.

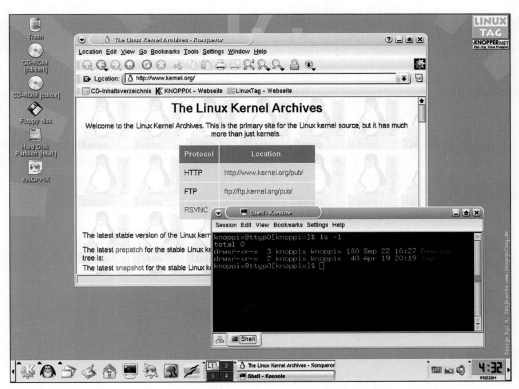

Figure 1.26

Example of one of the versions of the Linux operating system

Utility Programs

What are utility programs? Operating system software is the most critical software on the computer, because nothing can run without it. However, utility programs are another important component of system software. These small applications handle many important tasks involved with the management and maintenance of your system. Utility programs can be used to help back up important files, remove unwanted files or programs from your system, and schedule various tasks to keep your system running smoothly. Some of these utilities are included with the operating system, whereas others are stand-alone versions that you can purchase or download for free. The table in Figure 1.27 displays a variety of utility programs that ship with the Windows operating system and compares them with similar stand-alone products, describing the function of each utility.

Windows Utility Programs

Program	Function
Windows Explorer	Create folders, manage files, and compress/extract files. Read disk drive's properties including view storage capacity and free disk space, check drive for errors, defragment utility, and back up/restore utility
Windows Task Manager (Ctrl + Alt+ Delete)	Lets the user view the list of active applications, and switch or end any of them. Also, check the performance of the computer including CPU usage, RAM availability, and network utilization
Control Panel	
• System and Security	Review your computer's status Back up your computer Find and fix problems
• Network and Internet	View network status and tasks Choose home group and sharing options
• Hardware and sound	View devices and printers Add a device Connect to a projector Adjust commonly used mobility settings
• Programs	Install/uninstall programs Add desktop gadgets
• User Accounts and Family Safety	Add or remove user accounts Set up parental controls for any user
• Appearance and Personalization	Change the theme Change desktop background Adjust screen resolution
• Clock, Language, and Region	Change keyboards or other input methods Change display language Let Windows suggest settings
• Ease of Access	Optimize visual display
Administrative Tools	Schedule tasks
Security	
• Security Configuration Manager	Set account policies, local policies, network list manager policies, software restriction policies, and application control policies
• Firewall and Advanced Security	Set firewall and advanced security on local computer

Figure 1.27
Windows utility programs

Application Software

Application software or applications are comprised of programs that enable you to accomplish tasks and use the computer in a productive manner. Applications are programs created to perform a specific task, solve a specific problem, or address a specific need.

How do system software and application software work together? System software is like the breathing you need to do to live; however, you don't usually think much about it unless something goes wrong. Application software might be compared to a musical instrument like a flute. When a musician combines each of these breaths and her flute, the result may be a beautiful melody (if she has practiced, of course!). Computer software works together similarly; the system software acts as the "breath," while the application software provides the "instrument," enabling you to create something.

There are many different kinds of application software, although they often fall into one of several general categories, each of which has a different purpose. These categories include financial and business-related software, graphics and multimedia software, educational and reference software, entertainment software, and communication software. You might be most familiar with productivity software, which includes the following applications.

- ***Word processing software*** is used to create, edit, format, print, and save documents and other text-based files. Word processing software enables you to create or edit letters, reports, memos, and many other types of written documents that you can print or attach to an e-mail message. Revisions to existing documents can be made quickly and easily, without having to re-create the entire document. Documents created with this type of software can also include pictures, charts, ***hyperlinks,*** and other graphic elements. A hyperlink is a connection to another area of a document or a connection to an Internet URL. Microsoft Word, Lotus Word Pro, and Corel WordPerfect are all examples of word processing programs. A document created using Microsoft Word 2007 is shown in Figure 1.28. Notice that the document

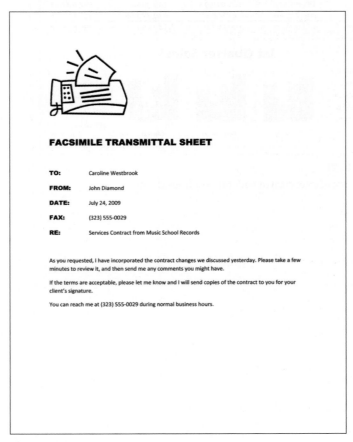

Figure 1.28
Sample document created with Microsoft Word 2007

contains a graphic element as well as text. Using word processing software replaces the use of conventional typewriters, on which editing was virtually impossible once the document was finished.

- ***Spreadsheet software*** enables the user to enter data in rows and columns format and:
  - Perform calculations on numeric data with user-defined formulas.
  - Convert part of the data into one or more charts, such as a column chart, a pie chart, or a line chart.
  - Work with lists to organize data and sort it in alphabetic or numeric order.
  - Create different scenarios and perform "what-if" analyses, the basis for sound decision making.

A key advantage of spreadsheet software is its capability to recalculate spreadsheets without user intervention. When data used in a calculation or a formula is changed, the spreadsheet software automatically updates the worksheet with the correct result. Microsoft Excel, Lotus 1-2-3, and Corel Quattro Pro are examples of spreadsheet programs. Figure 1.29 shows a worksheet and a chart created with Microsoft Excel 2007. The use of spreadsheet software replaces the old manual method of entering data in ledgers or journals and using a desktop calculator to do the math computations.

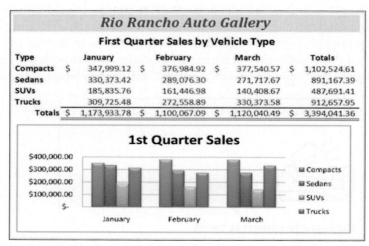

Figure 1.29

Example spreadsheet created with Microsoft Excel 2007

A database is a collection of data or unorganized facts. ***Database software*** is used to store, organize, update, and retrieve large amounts of data. ***Relational database software (RDBMS)*** stores information in tables, which enable users quick access to the data by connecting tables with common fields. ***Data mining*** is a function in some databases that looks for hidden patterns in the data to anticipate future patterns. This is commonly used in scientific applications and as a marketing tool to predict future consumer trends. Typically, database software can be used to manage various types of information, such as that found in large mailing lists, inventories, students' records, order histories, and invoicing. Databases help you to enter, store, sort, filter, retrieve, and summarize the information they contain and then generate meaningful reports. Common database programs include Microsoft Access, Lotus Approach, and Corel Paradox. Figure 1.30 shows a database object created in Microsoft Access 2007. Database software replaces an old manual filing system where information is stored in filing cabinets in a single location.

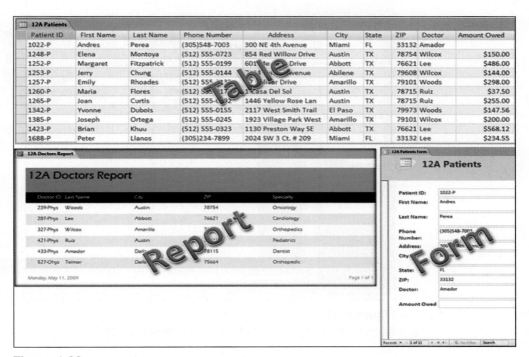

Figure 1.30
Examples of database software objects

Presentation software has become a standard in replacing flip charts, slide projectors, or overhead transparencies used by speakers and lecturers. This software is used to create electronic slides and project slide shows to visually present materials and ideas to large groups in a conference room or on the Web. Presentation software is also used to create audience handouts, speaker notes, and other materials that can be used during an oral presentation or for distribution to a group of participants. Microsoft PowerPoint, Lotus Freelance Graphics, and Corel Presentations are examples of presentation software programs. Figure 1.31 shows a presentation created with Microsoft PowerPoint 2007.

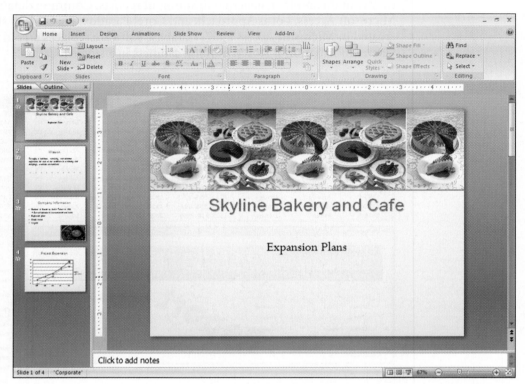

Figure 1.31
Example presentation created with Microsoft PowerPoint 2007

Communication and organizational software—Communication software can cover a broad range of tasks including videoconferencing and telephony. However, applications in the productivity category are most often used to send and receive e-mail. These applications typically include an address book (contacts list), a scheduler, a calendar, and task functions, which help users organize their personal and professional responsibilities. Microsoft Outlook, Lotus Notes, and Corel WordPerfect Mail are examples of communication and organizational software. Figure 1.32 shows an example of a calendar in Microsoft Outlook 2007.

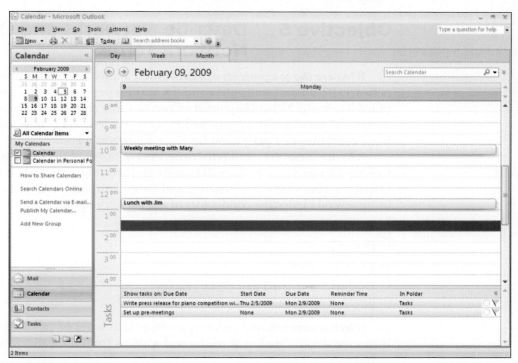

Figure 1.32

Example of a calendar in Microsoft Outlook 2007

What is a software suite? Although it is possible to buy any of the previous applications separately, most software manufacturers, including Microsoft, Corel, and Lotus, also group applications together into a package called a ***suite***. There is an alternative suite called OpenOffice and it's free. It is designed as an open source software in such a way that users can report bugs, request new features, or change and improve the software.

Another advantage of using a suite is that because products from the same company have many common elements, such as basic window design and layout, toolbars containing similar tools, dictionaries, and media galleries, many users find this familiarity makes it easier to switch between the programs in a suite. Examples of suites include Microsoft Office, Corel WordPerfect Office, and Lotus SmartSuite.

What are some other common software applications? As mentioned earlier, there are many different types of application software besides productivity software, each one with a specific function. Some of these are the following:

• You might use Microsoft Publisher or QuarkXPress to create newsletters or brochures.

• Bookkeepers rely on special accounting packages such as Peachtree Accounting or QuickBooks to balance the books and handle other accounting functions.

• Graphic designers turn to packages such as Adobe Photoshop or Adobe Illustrator to develop creative artwork.

• You might use Microsoft Expression Web or Macromedia Dreamweaver to create your own Web site.

- **IM** (instant messaging) software enables users to communicate in real time like a phone conversation but using text only. The software can alert you if a member of your group is online at that moment.
- Web browsers are software used to locate and display Web pages and navigate through them. They also enable users to store their frequently used sites for quick access.

If you have a specific need, chances are there is software that will address those needs. Today the best way to find software is to do a Web search using a search engine.

Objective 5 | Describe Networks and Define Network Terms

What are the components of a network? Connecting one computer to another creates a network. Recall that computers and the various peripherals that are connected to them are called hardware. Networks consist of two or more connected computers plus the various peripheral devices that are attached to them. Each object connected to a network, whether it is a computer or a peripheral device, is known as a ***node***.

Why are computers connected to networks? Some of the benefits of computer networks include the capability to share data, software, and resources such as printers, scanners, Internet access, video conferencing, and VoIP. Computers can be connected to a network using several media, the conductors of the network signals:

- Existing telephone wires
- Power lines
- Coaxial cables
- Unshielded twisted pair (UTP) cables
- Fiber optic

Wireless networks use radio waves instead of wires or cables to connect. Most networks use a combination of media and wireless communications (see Figure 1.33).

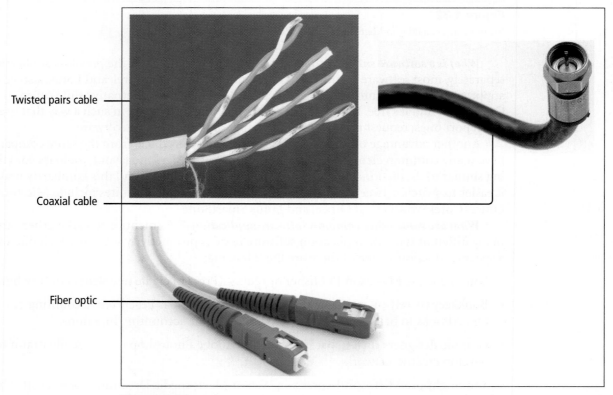

Twisted pairs cable

Coaxial cable

Fiber optic

Figure 1.33
Network media, the conductor of network signals

Today, using computer networks, institutions are able to *video conference*, that is, communicate audio and/or video between two or more individuals in different locations, optimizing communications, information sharing, and decision making.

Voice over Internet Protocol (*VoIP*) enables voice, facsimile, and voice-messaging communications over networks and the Internet.

Can networks be different sizes? A network that connects computers reasonably close together, say within a few city blocks in adjacent buildings, is called a *local area network (LAN).* See Figure 1.34.

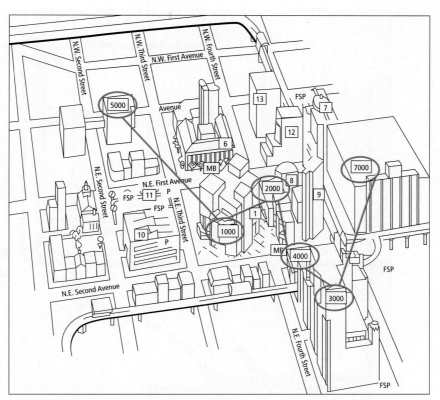

Figure 1.34
Example of a local area network, a college campus network that covers several buildings within a few city blocks

If the network grows to cover a larger geographic area or begins to include other networks, it becomes a **wide area network (WAN)**. An example is a state college campus that connects its computers with a LAN while all of its campuses connected together form a WAN. Because the different campuses are connected through WANs, students, faculty, staff, and administrators can easily and seamlessly use the resources of the entire network. Both LANs and WANs can be wired, wireless, or a combination of both. See Figure 1.35. The Internet is actually the largest WAN because it connects computer networks all around the world.

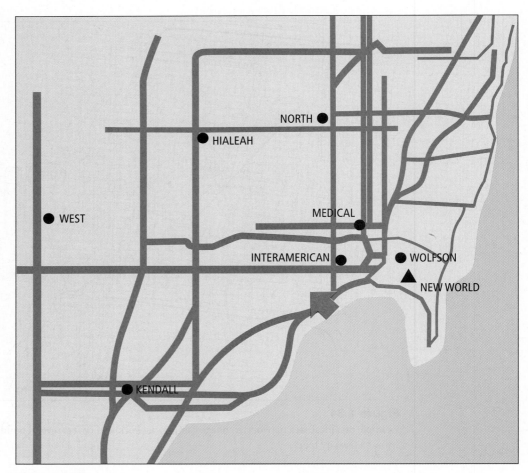

Figure 1.35
Example of a wide area network, which is a college network that links campus LANs in several cities within a county

Are networks public or private? They can be either. If you want to post information and make it available to any user, you post it on a website with no restrictions. If you want to protect certain information, you create an **intranet** in which access is restricted to authorized users only. Within an intranet, network administrators can limit the specific rights and privileges of different users.

How are networks configured? Networks can be configured in several ways. There are two main categories: peer-to-peer and client/server. **Peer-to-peer** or **P2P networks** are most commonly found in homes and small businesses. In a peer-to-peer network, each node can communicate with every other node without a dedicated server or hierarchy among computers. Peer-to-peer networks are relatively easy to set up, but tend to be rather small. This makes them ideal for home use, although not as desirable in the workplace. If a network grows to more than, say, ten to fifteen nodes, it is generally best to use the **client/server network**. In a client/server network, the server manages and controls all network resources. A node can be a computer, printer, scanner, modem, an external hard disk, or any other peripheral device connected to a computer. Therefore, it isn't difficult to find more than ten nodes in an office or business setting.

How is a client/server network different from a P2P network? Client/server networks typically have two different types of computers. The *client* is the computer used at your desk or workstation to write letters, send e-mail, produce invoices, or perform any of the many tasks that can be accomplished with a computer. The client computer is the one most people directly interact with. In contrast, the server computer is typically kept in a secure location and is used by network technicians and administrators to manage network resources. If a server is assigned to handle only specific tasks, it is known as a *dedicated server.* For instance, a Web server is used to store and deliver Web pages, a file server is used to store and archive files, and a print server manages the printing resources for the network. Each of these is a dedicated server.

As a client/server network grows in number of nodes and geographical distance covered, servers are assisted by distance-spanning devices such as switches and routers to optimize data traffic.

Network topology describes the different types of network architecture used for client/server networks (see Figure 1.36). Just as there are different sizes and styles of buildings that are designed for different purposes, networks are designed to be physically configured and connected in different ways.

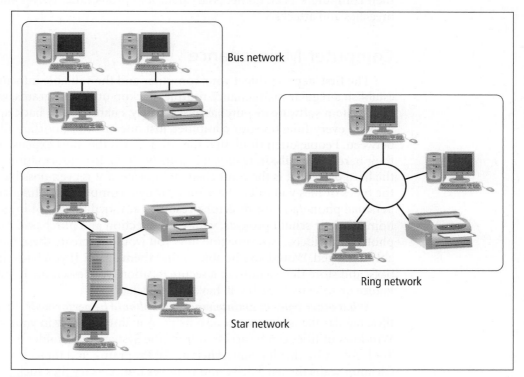

Figure 1.36
Common network topologies

Which topologies are used most often? The three most common layouts are explained in the following list:

- **Bus topology** connects each node to a single, central high-speed line known as a bus. No server is used, and although it is possible for each node to communicate with all the others, they can only do so one at a time. If one computer or device is sending over the network, all the others must wait until the transmission is complete before they can begin. Because this is an inexpensive and easy way to connect, this topology is often found in peer-to-peer networks.

- **Ring topology**, sometimes known as **token-ring topology**, connects each node to the next, forming a loop or a circle. The data that's sent is passed from node to node, traveling around the circle in only one direction. A token travels around the ring until one of the nodes is ready to send a transmission. The node then holds the token until the transmission is finished, preventing any of the other devices from sending until the token is released to make its way around the circle again. This type of topology gives each device an equal chance of being able to send data and prevents one node from doing all the communicating. This topology is being retired in favor of star topology.

- **Star topology** is the most frequent networking style used for businesses and homes. It offers a high degree of flexibility. Each node is connected to a special device known as a switch, which is centrally located. Each node must go through the switch to communicate with the others. If something happens to one node, the others are still able to communicate.

Objective 6 | Identify Safe Computing Practices

Being computer fluent implies you are a responsible computer user. This means more than just understanding the key components of a computer or the differences between hardware and software. Responsible computer users also know how to properly maintain their computers, back up necessary data, and protect themselves and others from security breaches and attacks.

Computer Maintenance

The first step to protect your computer and the valuable information it contains is to establish a regular maintenance routine. Backup utility programs, which may be part of your system software or purchased separately, enable you to back up your files. You can back up everything on your computer, just one or two important files, or anything in between. People often think that the computer is the most expensive item to replace if their hard drive fails. In reality, it is usually all the lost information that was contained on the hard drive that is the most costly to replace, if it is even possible to do so. Think about the types of files you might have on your own computer like financial records, your personal phone/address directory, resumes, scanned images of important documents, homework or school projects, your CD collection and purchased music files, and family photos and videos. Now imagine how you would re-create these files if they were irretrievably damaged. Would you be able to find them again? If you back up files on a regular basis and store the backups in a secure location, you lessen the impact that a mechanical failure or security breach will have on your data.

What other types of maintenance tasks should be performed? In addition to backing up files, regular file maintenance also helps to maintain order in your system. Several useful Windows utilities can be accessed from the System Tools folder. You can access the System Tools folder by clicking Start, clicking All Programs, and then clicking Accessories. Disk Cleanup scans the hard drive and removes unnecessary files such as those found in the Recycle Bin, in addition to temporary Internet files and other temporary files created by various programs. It is possible to adjust the settings and select which files to delete and which files to retain.

Similarly, the Disk Defragmenter scans the hard drive. However, rather than removing files, it attempts to reallocate files so they use the available hard drive space more efficiently. Recall that data is stored on hard drives in sectors and tracks. As file sizes change, they can outgrow their original location. When that happens, the remaining portion of the file may be stored elsewhere. If a file size decreases, or a file is deleted, this can create a blank area on the hard drive. Defragmenting a hard drive enables scattered portions of files to be regrouped and open spaces to be rearranged. This results in faster and more efficient file access, which improves the response time of the hard drive.

Is there a way to automate these maintenance tasks? Running these programs can be time-consuming, especially when you want to use your computer for other tasks. It is also easy to forget to do these things on a regular basis. That is why newer versions of Windows include a Task Scheduler. This utility enables you to create a task and select the best time for each task to run, in addition to how often, which makes the whole process automatic. Figures 1.37 and 1.38 show the steps to follow to reach the Task Scheduler dialog box for Windows Vista users and Windows 7 users, respectively.

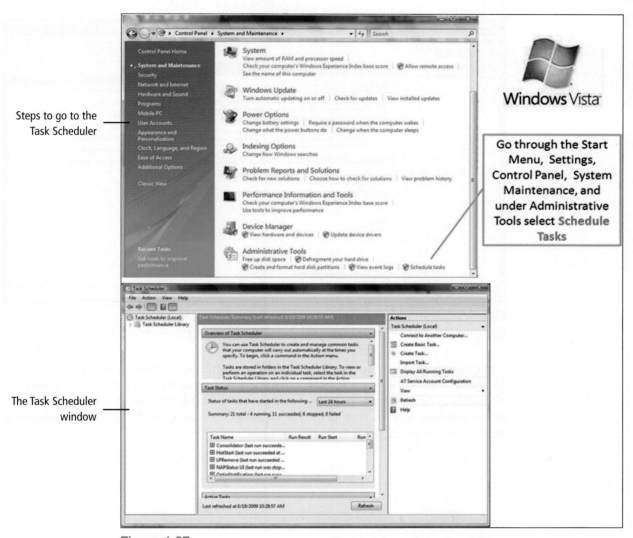

Steps to go to the Task Scheduler

The Task Scheduler window

Figure 1.37
Computer maintenance—Task Scheduler (Windows Vista users)

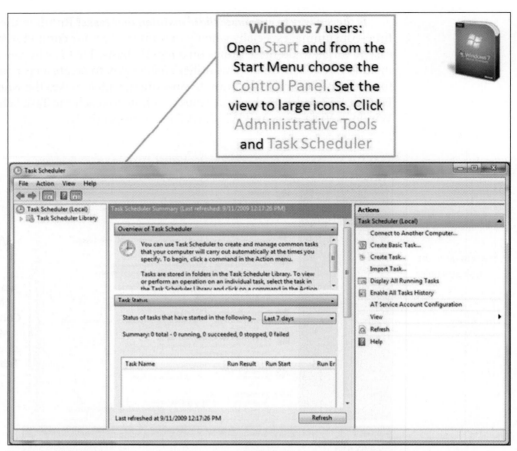

Figure 1.38
Computer maintenance—steps to set a task in the Task Scheduler (Windows 7 users)

Can changes to my system be undone? Sometimes when new software is installed on a computer, the results are not what you anticipated. Instead of playing a new game, you find your system stops responding each time you start it. Or, you might find the new driver you installed for your printer is causing conflicts. Even though you've tried to uninstall the software, the system is still not right.

Fortunately, if you are running a newer version of Windows, the System Restore utility come to the rescue. Periodically, Windows creates a ***restore point***, which records all the settings for your system. It's similar to taking a picture of how everything is currently set up. Figures 1.39 and 1.40 show steps to create a restore point for Windows Vista and Windows 7 users, respectively.

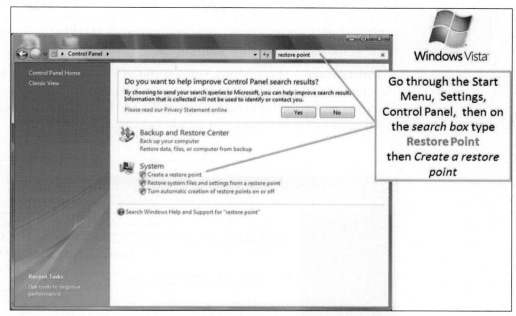

Figure 1.39

Computer maintenance—steps to create a Restore Point (Windows Vista users)

Figure 1.40

Computer maintenance—steps to create a Restore Point (Windows 7 users)

It is also possible to set manual restore points, and it is highly recommended that you set one before installing new software or hardware, or when making any major changes to your system. If you experience a problem with your system after the new software is installed, you can roll your system back to an earlier restore point when the system was working correctly. Think of it as an Undo button for your operating system. The good news is, returning to an earlier restore point affects only your system settings. It does not delete any of the data files you may have created during the interval.

What other functions can you use to maintain a "healthy" computer? Following are some of the other things that keep computers healthy:

- **Disk Cleanup**—This is a group of tasks intended to free disk space cause by Internet temporary files and hard drive unwanted files that accumulate from time to time. Part of this routine includes emptying the Recycle Bin. Figures 1.41 and 1.42 show the steps for accessing Disk Cleanup in Windows Vista and Windows 7.

Figure 1.41

Computer maintenance—steps to access Disk Cleanup (Windows Vista users)

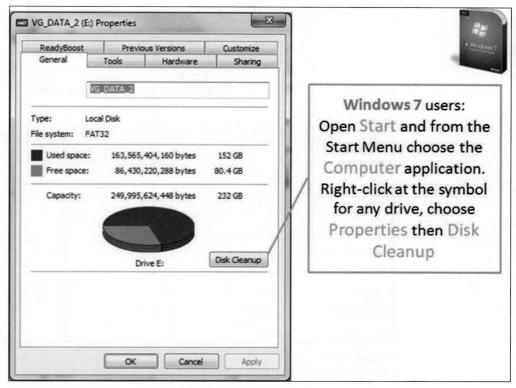

Figure 1.42
Computer maintenance—steps to access Disk Cleanup (Windows 7 users)

- **Activate and set up the Internet Pop-up Blocker**—This lets the user the select options to allow or to block advertising and other pop-up windows while surfing the Net. Figures 1.43 and 1.44 show the steps for accessing Pop-up Blocker in Windows Vista and Windows 7.

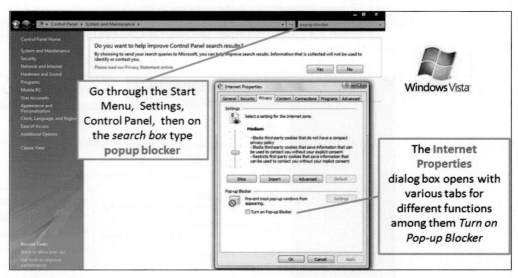

Figure 1.43
Computer maintenance—steps to access the Pop-up Blocker (Windows Vista users)

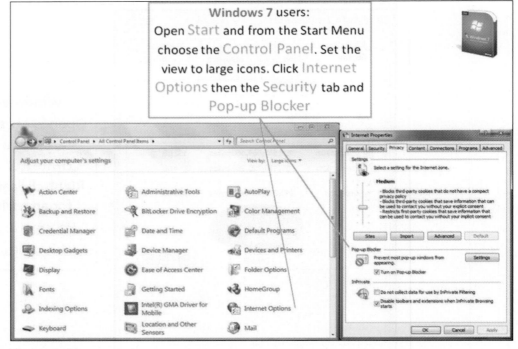

Figure 1.44
Computer maintenance—steps to access the Pop-up Blocker (Windows 7 users)

- **Access and set up Security settings**—You can set security settings, such as:

  - Check for security updates

  - Select the settings for the Windows Firewall

  - Check for Windows software updates

  - Scan for spyware and other potentially unwanted software

  - Change Internet security options

  Figures 1.45 and 1.46 show the steps for accessing security settings in Windows Vista and Windows 7.

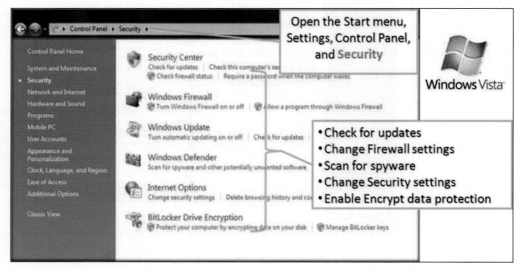

Figure 1.45
Computer maintenance—steps to access the Security settings (Windows Vista users)

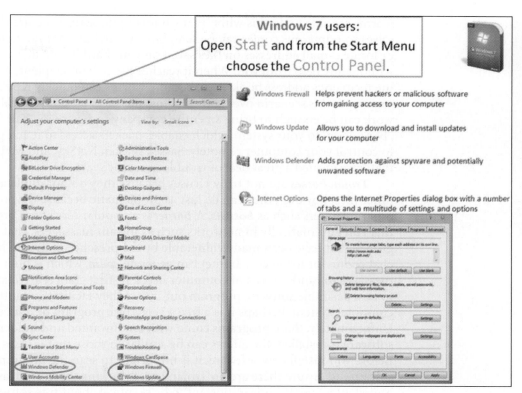

Figure 1.46
Computer maintenance—steps to access the Security settings and other functions (Windows 7 users)

Viruses

Establishing the habit of performing regular maintenance on your computer is one way to protect it, and yourself, from data loss. But there are many other dangers you need to be aware of too. Viruses, spyware, and **hackers** are all out there waiting to pounce on the unwary computer user. The term *hacker*, as used here, signifies an expert in computers and programming languages who uses his/her expertise to obtain unauthorized access to computer systems with the purpose corrupting data and/or stealing information.

What are viruses and how do they get on the computer? Computer **viruses** are malicious codes or software designed to invade your computer system and alter or destroy data without your knowledge and against your wishes. The severity of a virus can vary. Some viruses merely seem to be nuisances or might not even be obvious to the user; some cause files to be corrupted or erased; and others are capable of shutting down a computer and erasing the entire hard drive. Viruses infect a system and then attach themselves to a program or file to spread to other users.

Viruses can be distributed in several ways. In the early days of computers, viruses were spread by sharing infected floppy disks. Now, due to the ease in which files can be shared over the Internet, viruses are able to spread much more quickly. One of the most common ways to send a virus is through e-mail attachments. Security experts recommend that you never open an e-mail attachment unless you have first scanned it with antivirus software to determine that it is virus-free. Experts also recommend that unless you know the sender and have been expecting the e-mail attachment, it is best to delete the attachment without ever opening it. File-sharing services are another source for these types of problems.

Are viruses and worms the same thing? **Worms** are similar to viruses because they are also malicious programs that spread from computer to computer; however, unlike viruses, worms are able to do this without any human interaction and are able to replicate themselves so numerous copies can be sent. Worms can burrow into your e-mail address book, or locate e-mail addresses on files saved on your hard drive, then send themselves out without any help from you. When it reaches the e-mail recipient, it does the same thing to the recipient's address book. Also, because worms can quickly replicate themselves, they can repeat this scenario over and over. Just the sheer amount of traffic they cause on a network can be enough to bring an entire company to a grinding halt. Worms can also open a "back door" to your system, which enables hackers access to it and gives them the ability to control your computer remotely. Sasser, Blaster, NetSky, and MyDoom are all worms that have created a great deal of trouble in recent years.

Trojan horses are not truly viruses because they do not duplicate themselves or infect other files; however, they can be just as problematic because they open your system for other intruders such as **botnets**. A **botnet** is a popular term for a group of software robots that run automatically in networks such as instant massagers, chat rooms, and discussion groups that have been made vulnerable by the presence of Trojan horses. Once inside a chat room, for instance, a botnet can generate **spam,** which is bulk unsolicited e-mail messages to random lists of computer users. At first glance, a Trojan horse often appears to be a desirable software program but in fact they facilitate unauthorized access to a computer system. Perhaps it is a free screensaver program or a set of animated cursors. Unfortunately, these programs come with an unwanted and hidden agenda. After the software is installed, the effects can be similar to those that viruses or worms cause. Before you install new software, it is important to scan the program files with antivirus software to ensure there are no Trojan horses lurking there. And, as with unknown e-mail attachments, it is important to be skeptical about free software; it's not often that you really get something for nothing!

Spyware

How is spyware different from viruses? **Spyware** is software designed to capture personal and confidential information that resides on your system and send it elsewhere. It has quickly become as large a problem as viruses. Spyware's primary threat is to your privacy and confidentiality. Although spyware is not usually intended to harm your system, it can sometimes have that effect on it. **Adware** is spyware that tracks your Internet browsing and can install malicious cookies on your computer. A **cookie** is a small text file that contains information that can identify you to a website. Cookies are not necessarily bad. They are useful when they are used to help personalize your Web browsing experience, but cookies can threaten your privacy if they are used to reveal too much information.

How can you tell if spyware is on a computer? One symptom that indicates adware is on a computer is an increase in the number of pop-up ads the user receives, some of which might even address the user by name! Adware can generate pop-up ads even when you're not online. Some types of adware can also reset a Web browser's home page to a page of its choosing and take control of the search engine, directing you to websites that have been predetermined by the adware.

Are there other privacy threats? **Key loggers** are another type of spyware. In this case, a software program records every keystroke made on the computer. Key loggers can capture all sorts of confidential information this way—passwords, credit card numbers, bank account numbers, and so on—and then relay this information elsewhere. Entire e-mail messages and instant messaging conversations can be recorded this way too. Some key loggers are hardware, rather than software, although they perform the same devious function. Such hardware devices can be attached between the keyboard and the computer. The information stolen through the use of key loggers can easily make you a victim of identity theft. Trojan horses can be used to distribute key loggers and other types of spyware just as easily as they deliver viruses.

How can you avoid being a victim? To minimize the risk of having spyware installed on your computer, there are some practical precautions you can take. One of the most prevalent methods of spreading spyware is through file-sharing services, such as Morpheus or Kazaa. Not only can the file-sharing software include spyware, but often the files you think you are downloading for free are infected too. Although it's tempting to get the newest song or video for free from such a site, don't risk it!

This problem can be avoided if you use one of the legitimate, pay-as-you-go file-sharing services such as iTunes or the reincarnated Napster. Do not trust files or software sent by friends or acquaintances. Additionally, be cautious when you download and install freeware or shareware software. Make sure you deal with a reputable software publisher, scan the downloaded software for viruses and spyware, and read the licensing agreement. Some licensing agreements actually include information about additional software that will be automatically installed if you accept it.

Another way to prevent spyware is to avoid pop-up and banner ads whenever possible. You should never click on them. Often the "No Thanks" button is just a ruse to get you to click it and enable the spyware installation. Close pop-up ads by clicking the Close button in the top right corner. Installing pop-up blocking software can help to eliminate this risk almost entirely.

If you are running the most recent version of Windows, you already have a pop-up blocker available to you. You can view the pop-up blocker settings for Windows Vista in Figure 1.43 and access this dialog box through Internet Explorer's Tools menu. Many popular search engines, such as Google and Yahoo!, also include pop-up blocking features in their toolbars, which you can download at no charge. It is also wise to avoid questionable websites, because some of them can install spyware on your system just by visiting the site.

Protecting Yourself and Your Computer

In addition to being cautious in your Internet travels, there are some proactive measures you can take to protect yourself and your computer from viruses and spyware. These include:

- ***Software updates*** and ***patches***—Keeping your operating system and software up to date is critical. Software manufacturers are constantly on the lookout for security threats, and they issue updates and patches to help protect your system. Check for these and install them regularly. Software manufacturers have begun to implement automated procedures to check and install such updates. If your computer has this capability, it's a good idea to use this feature.

- ***Antivirus and antispyware software***—***Antivirus software*** is a utility program used to search your hard drive and files for viruses, and remove those that are found. ***Antispyware software*** works in a similar fashion, but searches for spyware rather than viruses. No computer should be without this protection. Many users erroneously think that because they aren't regularly online or use only a slow dial-up connection, they aren't a target. Nothing could be further from the truth! Recent studies show more than two-thirds of all computer users have some form of virus or spyware on their system.

There are a variety of antivirus and antispyware products available. Unfortunately, there are also a lot of dishonest companies purporting to offer these products. Too often, these are really scams that will actually install spyware or viruses on your system! To avoid being scammed or downloading something malicious, you should never respond to offers that are received in a pop-up ad or unsolicited e-mail. To obtain legitimate products, it is best to purchase them from the manufacturer's website or from a local retailer. Additionally, some internet service providers are beginning to provide some of these products as part of their services.

Some well-known antivirus products include Norton AntiVirus (*www.symantec.com*), McAfee VirusScan (*www.mcafee.com*), and AVG Anti-Virus (*www.grisoft.com*).

Antispyware products include eTrust PestPatrol (*www.pestpatrol.com*), Ad-Aware (*www.lavasoft.com*), and Spybot Search & Destroy (*www.safer-networking.org*). You can search for other products at popular download sites such as Download.com (*www.download.com*) or Tucows (*www.tucows.com*) but you should be sure to read the software reviews and evaluate their usefulness before downloading or installing them.

It is best to use only one antivirus product, because running more than one can cause conflicts between the programs. However, because there are so many different types of spyware, antispyware products may address these problems in different ways. Experts recommend running at least two different antispyware applications in order to catch as many spyware programs as possible. It's not enough to install antivirus and antispyware software on your system; you need to update it frequently, at least once a week. Doing so will protect you against any new viruses or spyware created since the last time you checked. Software should be set to scan incoming data files, e-mail, and so on but regular full-system scans should be conducted on a weekly basis as well.

Personal firewalls—Firewalls may be software programs or hardware devices, although their purpose is the same to prevent unauthorized access to your computer. When a firewall is installed properly, it can make your computer invisible to hackers and other invaders. Not only can a good firewall help prevent infections and identity theft; it can also prevent hackers from accessing your computer and turning it into a ***zombie***. A zombie computer is one that can be controlled remotely and can be used to help spread viruses, spyware, or junk e-mail known as spam. Zombie computers can also be used in ***denial of service (DoS)*** attacks. DoS attacks occur when a large number of computers try to access a website at the same time, effectively overloading it and causing it to shut down. If you are using Windows XP or Windows Vista, you already have a firewall available to you.

You can access the firewall settings by clicking the Start button, settings, Control Panel, Security, and Windows Firewall.

What else should I look for? It might sound simple, but when online, do not give out personal information unless it is for legitimate purposes. It is important to avoid spam e-mail and ***phishing*** attacks e-mails that masquerade as authentic entities, such as banks and credit card companies, and ask for confidential information. Legitimate organizations will not ask for passwords, bank account numbers, or credit card details through e-mail. It is also possible to check for hoaxes and scams at a variety of websites, including many of the antivirus and antispyware sites. When in doubt, do some research to see if the request you've received is legitimate. If necessary, make a telephone call to the agency in question. Viewing such requests with a critical eye can help you avoid online scams and hoaxes.

Content-Based Assessments

Content-Based Assessments

Matching

A Application
   software

B Computer

C Computer network

D Console/system
   unit

E CPU

F Hardware

G DVDs or CDs

H Memory (RAM)

I Motherboard/
   system board

J Peripherals

K Port

L Server

M Software

N Spyware

O Topology

Match each term in the second column with its correct definition in the first column. Write the letter of the term on the blank line in front of the correct definition.

_____ 1.   Computer programs.

_____ 2.   Programs that enable you to accomplish a specific tasks or solve a specific need.

_____ 3.   Two or more computers connected together to enable resource sharing.

_____ 4.   Used to manage network resources, this type of computer can be dedicated to a specific task.

_____ 5.   Optical disk drives use this type of storage media.

_O_ 6.   The layout or design/arrangement of computers connected to a network.

_K_ 7.   A peripheral device uses this to attach to the computer.

_B_ 8.   A programmable electronic device that can input, process, output, and store data.

_F_ 9.   The physical components of a computer system.

_J_ 10. Hardware connected outside the computer's system unit.

_D_ 11. The hardware unit that typically contains the CPU, RAM, a hard disk, and a power supply.

_I_ 12. A large printed circuit board to which all the other components are connected.

_____ 13. The temporary storage that holds data and instructions waiting to be processed.

_E_ 14. The processing unit.

_____ 15. This type of program threatens a user's privacy.

Multiple Choice

Circle the correct response.

1. Which of the following requires one byte of storage?
    a. Page
    b. Paragraph
    c. Sentence
    d. Character

2. Which of the following units represents the fastest CPU clock speed?
    a. 733 MHz
    b. 286 MHz
    c. 2 GHz
    d. 2 GB

3. Which of the following is not an input device?
    a. Keyboard
    b. Speaker
    c. Mouse
    d. Stylus

4. Which of the following is an example of optical storage media?
    a. Disk drive
    b. Flash card
    c. RAM
    d. Compact disc

5. Which of the following is not a type of computer?
    a. Mainframe
    b. Multitask
    c. Server
    d. Supercomputer

6. Before a computer can process data, where must data be stored?
    a. In RAM
    b. On a disk
    c. In the control unit
    d. On the monitor

7. What term, related to computers, means billions?
    a. Byte
    b. Mega
    c. Giga
    d. Hertz

8. Which of the following is not a type of microcomputer?
    a. Desktop
    b. Notebook
    c. Personal digital assistant
    d. Microprocessor

9. Which of the following can prevent the easy and casual connection to your computer by a nonauthorized user?
    a. Disk defragmenter
    b. Antivirus software
    c. Firewall
    d. Key logger

10. Which of the following is capable of opening a "back door" on a computer and is able to spread without human interaction?
    a. Trojan horse
    B. Worm
    c. Adware
    d. Zombie

Glossary

Adware Spyware that tracks your Internet browsing and can install malicious cookies on your computer.

Antispyware software A utility program used to search your hard drive for spyware, and remove those that are found.

Antivirus software A utility program used to search your hard drive for viruses, and remove those that are found.

Application software Programs that accomplish specific tasks, such as word processing, photo editing, or sending e-mail, and using the computer in a productive manner.

Arithmetic logic unit (ALU) Handles addition, subtraction, multiplication, and division, and also makes logical and comparison decisions.

Arrow keys Keys located at the bottom right of the keyboard between the standard keys and the numeric keypad that enable the user to move the insertion point around the active window.

Audio port Similar to video ports, these ports connect audio devices, such as speakers, headphones, and microphones to the computer's sound card.

Backup tape drive A storage device used to save data to tape media resembling audiocassettes.

Bluetooth A type of wireless technology that relies on radio wave transmission and doesn't require a clear line of sight. It is typically limited to less than 30 feet.

Boot The process of starting up a computer; the computer begins when power is turned on.

Botnet Term associated with malicious software or software *robots*.

Browser See Web browser.

Burn The process that saves data by using a laser beam that burns tiny pits into the storage medium.

Bus topology In a computer network, it connects each node to a single, central high-speed line known as a bus.

CD Acronym for compact disk; a polycarbonate material with one or more metal layers capable of optically storing digital information.

CD burner Type of optical drive capable of reading and writing data from and to a CD (provided the media is recordable, like CD-Rs and CD-RWs).

CD drive Type of optical drive that can read CDs (compact disks).

CD-ROM CD media that was burned once and from that moment on can only be read.

CD-R Also known as CD-Recordable, a type of compact disk that can be recorded using a CD burner (drive).

CD-RW A rewritable disc that enables data to be recorded, revised, or deleted, and new data written to the disc, similar to magnetic media.

Central processing unit (CPU) The part of the computer responsible for controlling all the commands and tasks the computer performs, acting as the brain of the computer.

Click A mouse function in which you point at an object, press and release the left (or primary) mouse button once.

Client In a client/server network, the computer used at a desk or workstation to write letters, send e-mail, produce invoices, or perform any of the many tasks that can be accomplished with a computer.

Client/server network A network in which two different types of computers have different functions. See also Client and Server.

Clock speed A measure of the speed at which a CPU processes data (number of instructions per second).

Communication and organizational software A program such as Microsoft Outlook 2007, used to send and retrieve e-mail, manage day-to-day tasks such as appointments and contacts.

Compact disk See CD

Computer A programmable electronic device that can input, process, output, and store data.

Computer fluent Describes a person who understands the capabilities and limitations of computers and knows how to use computer technology to accomplish tasks.

Configure To put together by selecting a combination of components, features, and options.

Connectivity port Ports such as Ethernet and modem that are used to connect a computer to a local network or to the Internet.

Control keys Keys such as the Ctrl, Alt, and the Windows key that provide shortcuts or increased functionality to the keyboard when used in combination with other keys.

Control unit In the CPU, the component responsible for obtaining and executing instructions from the computer's memory.

Cookie A small text file that contains information that can identify you to a website.

CPU See Central processing unit

Data Represents text, numbers, graphics, sounds, and videos entered to the computer's memory during input operations.

Database software Programs, such as Microsoft Access 2007, used to store and organize large amounts of data and perform complex tasks such as sorting and querying to generate specialized reports.

Data mining A function is some database software that looks for hidden patterns in the data to anticipate future trends.

Dedicated server A server in a network that is assigned to handle only specific tasks.

Denial of service (DoS) Attacks that occur when a large number of computers try to access a website at the same time, effectively overloading it and causing it to shut down.

Desktop computer A class of microcomputer, such as a PC or a Mac, that typically occupies a working area around a desk.

Device A hardware component that attaches to a computer. Includes disk drives, printers, mice, keyboards, and modems.

Dialog box A frame or window that shows the presets or defaults for a specific function and enables the user to make changes before moving ahead.

Digital camera A device that stores pictures digitally rather than using conventional film.

Digital video recorder Devices that let you capture digital images and movies and transfer them directly to your computer.

Digital Video Interface (DVI) port Ports that transmit a pure digital signal, eliminating the need for digital-to-analog conversion and resulting in a higher quality picture on an LCD monitor.

Docking station Device that enables the user to connect a notebook to a full-size keyboard, monitor, and other devices in an office setting.

DOS The original OS for personal computers in the early 1980s. This was a text-based or keyboard-driven operating system.

Dot matrix Printers that have small hammers, similar to a typewriter's, that strike a ribbon against paper, leaving behind the image of a character or symbol.

Dot pitch A display characteristic in monitors that refers to the diagonal distance between two pixels of the same color. The smaller the dot pitch results in a crisper viewing image because there is less blank space between the pixels.

Dots per inch (dpi) How resolution is expressed. The higher the dpi, the better the print quality.

Double-click The action of clicking and releasing the left mouse button twice in rapid succession while keeping the mouse still.

Drag The action of moving something from one location on the screen to another; the action includes pointing and clicking (releasing the mouse button at the desired time or location).

DSL Acronym for digital subscriber line. Type of communications line in which signals travel through copper wires between a telephone switching station and a home or business.

Dual-boot A computer that can run more than one operating system.

Dual-core Processors that have several advantages over a single processor CPU, including improved multitasking capabilities, system performance, and lower power consumption.

DVD Acronym for Digital Video Disk or Diversified Video Disk; media that holds data written by an optical device.

DVD drive Digital Video Disk drive capable of reading and writing DVD media.

DVD-ROM DVD media that was burned once and from that moment on can only be read.

DVI port See Digital Video Interface.

Embedded computers Small specialized computers built into larger components such as automobiles and appliances.

Ethernet port A port, slightly larger than a telephone jack, that can transmit data at speeds up to 1,000 megabits per second (Mbps) and is usually used to connect to a cable modem or a network.

Firewall A combination of hardware and software used to prevent unauthorized access to your computer.

FireWire port A port used to send data at rates up to 800 megabits per second (Mbps), frequently used for digital cameras or digital video recorders.

Flash drive A small, portable, digital storage device that connects to a computer's USB port (Universal Serial Bus); also called a thumb drive, jump drive, or USB drive.

Flash memory Portable, nonvolatile memory that uses electronic, solid-state circuitry.

Flat-panel displays Flat-panel displays or LCD monitors that use a liquid crystal display and are thin and energy efficient.

Floppy diskette Magnetic media used for data storage.

Floppy disk drive Device used to read and write to floppy diskettes media.

Function keys Keys that are located above the standard row of number keys and numbered F1 through F12. These keys are generally associated with certain software-specific commands.

Gaming computers Computers that are mostly used by video game enthusiasts. They are usually configured with a fast CPU, large size memory, a special video card, sound card, and surround sound speaker system.

Gigabyte (GB) Approximately one billion bytes; a unit used to measure memory size and storage space.

Gigahertz (GHz) One billion hertz; a hertz is one of the units used to measure processor speed. One hertz is one cycle (instruction read) per second.

Graphical user interface (GUI) Today's operating systems provide a *user-friendly* way to operate a computer with their graphical user interface. The user controls the action using the keyboard, a mouse, or a touch screen to make selections from onscreen objects such as icons, menus, or dialog boxes.

GUI See Graphical user interface.

Hackers Derogatory term to describe individuals who gain unauthorized access to computer systems for the purpose of corrupting or stealing data.

Handheld computers Small portable computers that might include personal productivity software and enable the user to play music, take photos and video, make phone calls, and access the Internet. PDAs, Pocket PCs, and smart phones fall in this category.

Hard copy The output of a printer (synonymous with printout).

Hard disk drive A combination of a device and media used as the main storage in most computers.

Hardware The physical or tangible components of the computer and any equipment connected to it.

Hyperlink A connection to another area of a document or a connection to an Internet URL.

Icon A graphic representation of an object on the screen. Icons can be selected with the mouse or using your fingers on a touch screen.

IM Acronym for instant messaging, software that enables users to communicate in real time like a phone conversation but using text only.

Impact A type of printer that resembles a typewriter; a key punches an inked ribbon to imprint a characters on paper.

Information Data that has been organized in a useful manner.

Information processing cycle The cycle composed of the four basic computer functions: input, process, output, and storage.

Ink-jet A nonimpact printer that uses a special nozzle and ink cartridges to distribute liquid ink on the surface of the paper.

Input During this step of the information processing cycle, the computer gathers data or allows a user to enter data onto memory.

Input devices Computer hardware used to enter data and instructions into a computer; examples include the keyboard, mouse, stylus, scanner, microphone, and digital camera.

Insertion point A blinking vertical line on the screen that shows where the next typed character will appear.

Internet control key Typically located at the top of certain keyboards, these keys enable the user to assign to each key a unique Web browser functions such as sending e-mail, browsing a specific site, or accessing their online bank account.

Intranet A network or part of a network in which access is restricted to authorized users only.

IrDA port A port that is used to allow devices such as PDAs, keyboards, mice, and printers to transmit data wirelessly to another device by using infrared light waves.

Joysticks Game controls that are input devices used to control movement within video games.

Key logger A type of spyware that records every keystroke made on the computer and can capture all sorts of confidential information this way such as passwords, credit card numbers, bank account numbers, and so on.

Keyboard The primary input device for computers.

Kilobit One thousand bits. It takes eight bits to make one byte.

Kilobyte Approximately one thousand bytes.

LAN Acronym for local area network. A network that connects computers that are reasonably close together.

Laser printer A type of nonimpact printer that uses a drum, static electricity, and a laser to distribute dry ink or toner on the surface of the paper.

LightScribe A disc-labeling technology that burns text and graphics onto the surface of a specially coated LightScribe CD or DVD.

Linux An alternative operating system. It is open source software, which means it is not owned by a single company and some versions are available at no cost.

Liquid crystal display (LCD) Technology used in flat panel monitors, resulting in thinner, lighter monitors that consume less energy.

Local area network (LAN) A network in which the nodes are located within a small geographic area.

Mac OS An operating system designed specifically for Apple's Macintosh computers.

Magnetic A type of storage process using magnetized film to store data; used by devices such as hard disks, or media such as tape cartridges.

Mainframe computers Computers often found in large businesses, organizations, and government agencies where thousands of users need to simultaneously use the data and resources for their everyday operations.

Megabit (Mb) Approximately one million bits. It takes eight bits to make a byte.

Megabyte (MB) Approximately one million bytes; a unit of measure for memory and storage space.

Megahertz (MHz) One million hertz; a hertz is one of the units used to measure processor speed. One hertz is one cycle (instruction read) per second.

Memory A generic term that signifies storage.

Menu A list of commands that perform specific tasks within a program.

MFD Acronym for Multi-Function Devices.

Microcomputer The computer most users are familiar with and that ranges in size from large desktop systems to handheld devices. The name comes from its main component or brain called the "microchip" or microprocessor.

Microphones Input devices used to capture and record sounds.

Microprocessor chip A microcomputer's main component; it is a tiny but powerful chip compared to a mainframe or a supercomputer.

Microsoft Windows The operating system that runs most microcomputers today and provides a graphical user interface to make the computer "user friendly."

MIDI port Ports used to connect electronic musical devices, such as keyboards and synthesizers, to a computer.

Mobile devices These devices fall into the category of handheld computers; they are small enough to fit in the palm of your hand and enable users to access personal productivity software, send and read e-mail, navigate the Internet, and some are capable of wireless communications.

Modem port Ports used to connect a computer to a local network or to the Internet.

Monitor (or display screen) Display devices that show images of text, graphics, and video once data has been processed.

Monitor port A port that is used to connect the monitor to the graphics-processing unit, which is usually located on the motherboard or on a video card.

Motherboard A large printed circuit board located in the system unit to which all other boards are connected; the motherboard contains the central processing unit (CPU), the memory (RAM) chips, expansion card slots, and ports.

Mouse An input device (pointing device) used to enter commands and user responses into a computer. This device controls a symbol on the screen (mouse pointer) used to manipulate objects and select commands.

Mouse pointer In a graphical user interface environment, a pointer is a small arrow or other symbol on the screen that moves as you move the mouse. This lets the user make selections from objects on the screen such as icons, menus, or dialog boxes.

Multifunction device (MFD) Hardware devices such as All-in-One printers that provide a number of functions in one unit.

Multimedia control key Some modern keyboards have at least a few keys or buttons that can be used for such tasks as muting or adjusting speaker volume, opening a Web browser, and sending e-mail.

Multimedia projectors Output devices used to display information on a screen for viewing by a large audience.

Multitask To perform more than one task simultaneously.

Network A group of two or more computers (or nodes) connected together via cables or wirelessly, to share information and resources.

Network topology The layout and structure of a computer network.

Node Any object connected to a network that is a computer or a peripheral device.

Nonimpact Printers that generate hard copies by means other than striking elements on to a ribbon and paper. They do not touch the paper when printing.

Nonvolatile Permanent storage; type of storage that holds its contents even when power is shut down. "Read Only Memory" (ROM) is a type of permanent storage.

Notebook computer Also known as a laptop, this microcomputer is smaller than a desktop and designed to be portable.

Numeric keypad A cluster of keys located at the right of the keyboard. This provides an alternative method of quickly entering numbers.

Open-source An operating system not owned by any company and that can be changed by people with the appropriate programming knowledge.

Operating system (OS) The software that controls the way the computer works from the time it is turned on until it is shut down.

Optical A type of storage process that uses a laser to read and write data; used to burn media such as CDs and DVDs.

OS See Operating system.

Output Data that has been processed and converted into information.

Output device Computer hardware components used to display information (show it) to the user; examples include the monitor, printer, and speakers.

P2P network (Peer-to-peer) A type of network in which each node can communicate with every other node. No PC has control over the network.